iLOBBY.EU

iLOBBY.EU

Survival Guide to EU Lobbying, including the Use of Social Media

Caroline De Cock

Eburon Delft

2010

ISBN 978-90-5972-439-6 (paperback)
ISBN 978-90-5972-440-2 (ebook)

Eburon Academic Publishers
P/O Box 2867
2601 CW Delft
The Netherlands
Tel.: +31 (0)15 2131484 / Fax: +31 (0)15 2146888
info@eburon.nl / www.eburon.nl

Cover design: Textcetera

TABLE OF CONTENTS

PREFACE
LOBBYING: CHESS OR SOMETHING ELSE?

Being a lobbyist is not an obvious career choice, even for a Belgian living a stone's throw away from Brussels.

I started my professional life as a lawyer in the only field I could find that did not already boast huge layers of dust on its related legal books: the Internet.

In the course of a decade, my curiosity and professional opportunities led me from the Big Four[1] consulting world to a competition law firm and then to what insiders call the 'industry', i.e. big multinational telecommunications companies.

My passion for the Internet and technical matters which affect the daily lives of citizens and businesses around the globe has been the red thread in my career. What I enjoy the most as a lawyer is getting my head around technical and practical matters in order to raise the discussion to a different level. This has made me study late at night how websites are put together (even dabbing into PHP and HTML coding), just to be able to counter-argue when a webmaster or programmer would tell me one of my legally-motivated requests on a site was 'technically impossible' or too difficult. I did the same when it came to understanding how the Internet functions and annoyed more than one engineer by nagging them to show me places like 'Network Operation Centres' or opening pavements to see what fibre networks really looked like.

When I started as a freelance consultant, my main drive was to be able to pick and choose the issues I was going to work on - something in-house regulatory departments and multi-consultancy firms rarely allow you to do.

For a long time, I didn't consider myself a lobbyist, what with being a lawyer whose serious business card read 'Regulatory Policy'. Moreover, the term lobbyist was extremely rare in Brussels, almost as if it had a

---

[1] The Big Four are the four largest international accountancy and professional services firms, which handle the vast majority of audits for publicly traded companies as well as many private companies

dirty connotation: people would say they worked in EU affairs, PR, governmental relations, regulatory, compliance, think tanks... Anything except lobbying!

But a discussion with an American client made me realise that *that* was precisely what I was doing (and she claimed I was even good at it). I have since then decided to go beyond the negative connotation of the 'L word' and to carry the lobbying label with pride.

So, what exactly is lobbying? According to Wikipedia[2], *"Lobbying is the practice of influencing decisions made by government (in groups or individually). It includes all attempts to influence legislators and officials, whether by other legislators, constituents, or organized groups. A lobbyist is a person who tries to influence legislation on behalf of a special interest or a member of a lobby."*

I actually like this definition as it has the merit of recognising that lobbying is not only done by industry or trade associations, but by any organised group and even 'other legislators'. I am often amused when I see statements by bloggers or internet surfers saying: "Call your MEP to have law X change and fight against those nasty lobbyists!" Now, what exactly do they think they are encouraging others to do? It would certainly qualify as lobbying in my book.

When people, and in particular young students, ask what a lobbyist does, I compare the job to two things: marriage counselling and curling.

First, lobbyists are like marriage counsellors because their job involves listening, trying to understand how both sides see things and then subtly explaining why a specific perspective on a given issue should be preferred over another. The goal is to make everyone in the room feel like their views have been respected.

Secondly, while lobbying is often compared to a subtle game of chess, it actually has more in common with curling.

Imagine the following scene: Four players are awkwardly balancing on an ice skating rink lit only by bleak neon lights, somewhere in the middle of Canada. One of the men is holding a heavy-looking, polished oblong stone made of Scottish granite at arm's length. The aim of the game is to

---

[2] See http://en.wikipedia.org/wiki/Lobbying. The author acknowledges that Wikipedia is probably not the most trustworthy source of information but considers that in this case, the definition is one that reflects quite well reality, hence the choice to quote it.

slide the heavy rock across the slippery frozen surface and get it to halt as close as possible to a bull's eye target marked on the ice. The thrower receives help from a teammate shouting instructions from behind the end line several dozen feet away. Two other players, known as sweepers, start to furiously rub the ice in front of the rock with broomsticks in order to smooth the path.

If you're a continental European, the whole process might look similar to the French lawn game known as *pétanque* or *boules*. North Americans are likely to be reminded of a giant shuffleboard game. To me, however, curling has an awful lot in common with lobbying.

Just like the curler, the European Commission tosses a piece of weighty, not very attractive-looking legislation out into the field, and all the stakeholders start brushing to blaze the way for the brainless object to end up exactly where they want it to go. Good strategies and sound collaboration are essential in defining the trajectory of your lobbying efforts, and the skills of individual players will determine how close you get to the desired result. And, at the end of the day, success depends not only on skills, sweat and brains, but also on an element of luck.

iLobby.eu sets out how to lobby the EU from the perspective of an actual lobbyist sharing her experiences and anecdotes. It also looks at the use of Web 2.0 / social networking tools in the area of lobbying and politics, by giving practical overviews, examples of worst and best practices, as well as recommendations for politicians, PR and e-communications professionals, lobbyists and campaigners of all sorts.

I decided to write this book after discovering that many of my clients, as well as students I met at various seminars, were unable to find an easily accessible source to understand the functioning of the European institutions.

Another catalyst were the very positive responses received from readers of my blog www.lobbyplanet.eu (ranked in the 2010 top 3 of Euroblogs by Bloggingportal, the largest portal of EU blogs) and Twitter feed @linotherhino (ranked in the 2009 top 3 of EU influential Twitterers). It never ceases to amaze me that so few of my European lobbyist colleagues have yet picked up on the power inherent to all these new social networking and information sharing tools. Although they don't replace the 'old methods' of lobbying, they add essential new ways of interacting and gathering intelligence. Ignoring them could be detrimental to your business.

My book is aimed at lobbyists, activists, think thanks, journalists, students of political and social sciences, business administration or law, and anyone interested in understanding the way EU decision-making works and how lobbying is changing under the influence of social media. But it is a valuable source for business people with activities in Europe who wish to understand what their company should consider before hiring a lobbyist or devising its lobbying strategy.

As an avid EU lobbyist, I have had to learn the process through trial and error. There have been funny and even touching moments in my career, but also equally painful bruises (mostly to my ego). This book should go some way to show you the way to constructive lobbying and the successful use of social media and avoid pitfalls on the way there.

ACKNOWLEDGMENTS

This is oddly the most difficult part to write, as many people helped me in so many different ways.

But first things first: my husband Patrick and my three kids, David, Alex and Sofie. Their patience at accepting my sleepless writing nights and follow-up grumpy mornings has been exceptional. The fact that my writing a book made my kids say I was "cool" was probably the best reward I could ever dream of when embarking on this adventure. And Patrick's ongoing support for every new crazy idea I decide to pursue is just too tremendous for words.

I would also like to thank Emma Gilthorpe, who made me switch from legal affairs to EU affairs, a change I have never regretted since.

Still in the strong women section, I must acknowledge the impact of my mother, who has raised me to be what I am today, and supports me whatever I do.

This book has also benefitted from the helpful insights of Nina Lamparski, my tough but always so right reviewer and editor, Ronny Patz, an outstanding EU expert and euroblogger, and Herman Rucic, whose enthusiasm, support and constructive comments were greatly appreciated.

Finally, a book needs a publisher I was told and I must say Wiebe de Jager has been absolutely great, in accepting both to patiently listen to my wacky ideas for covers, to trust me on the content of the book and to push the limits to the extreme to publish as quickly as possible.

Thank you

Caroline De Cock

PART 1:
HOW TO LOBBY EUROPE
THE BASICS

" 'Lobbyist' has never been a good word. I grew up in Delaware, and I had to give a speech (...). There were about 50 guys who all knew my family very well, and I said, 'because of the work I do, I am a registered lobbyist, but please do not tell my mother. She still thinks I'm a piano player at a whorehouse and would be horrified to find out I was a lobbyist'"

Anonymous US lobbyist, "The lobbyist's book of quotes", by Ch. de Fouloy.

CHAP. 1: WHO?
THE INSTITUTIONAL TRIANGLE

I. INTRODUCTION

Who should you lobby in order to influence the European decision-making process in Brussels?

The question seems obvious enough but the answer is not always that simple, and can actually prove rather overwhelming.

In this part of the book, we will look at the institutional triangle (see Figure 1) involved in the legislative process at European level, to gain a better understanding of how to best push your agenda. They are:

- The Council of the European Union;

- The European Commission; and,

- The European Parliament.

They are examined in no particular order of importance as all three are equally important in the policy and legislative arenas (even if, when depicting the institutional triangle, the European Commission is commonly put at the top as it usually proposes legislation).

Of course, other institutions also intervene, but they either don't have as much impact on the final outcome, or are limited to very specialised fields. Think of advisory bodies such as the European Economic and Social Committee, and the Committee of the Regions; or specialised institutions like the European Court of Justice, European Investment Bank, or Court of Auditors. As a time-pushed (or budget constrained) lobbyist who needs to prioritise their targets, you might not have the time to reach out them.

As a result, the book will not focus on these bodies.

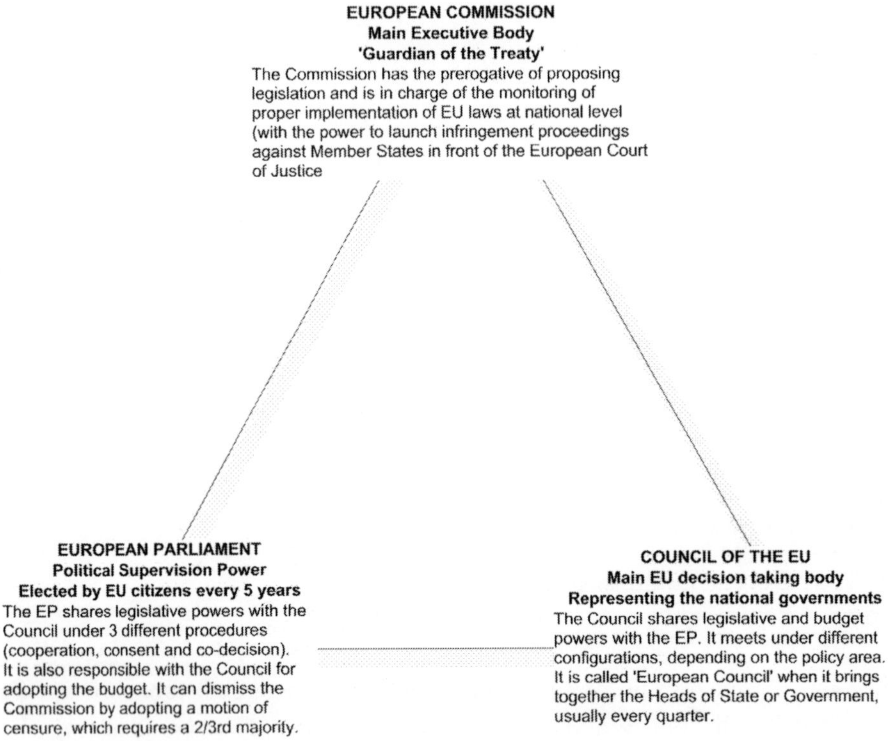

EUROPEAN COMMISSION
Main Executive Body
'Guardian of the Treaty'
The Commission has the prerogative of proposing
legislation and is in charge of the monitoring of
proper implementation of EU laws at national level
(with the power to launch infringement proceedings
against Member States in front of the European Court
of Justice

EUROPEAN PARLIAMENT
Political Supervision Power
Elected by EU citizens every 5 years
The EP shares legislative powers with the
Council under 3 different procedures
(cooperation, consent and co-decision).
It is also responsible with the Council for
adopting the budget. It can dismiss the
Commission by adopting a motion of
censure, which requires a 2/3rd majority.

COUNCIL OF THE EU
Main EU decision taking body
Representing the national governments
The Council shares legislative and budget
powers with the EP. It meets under different
configurations, depending on the policy area.
It is called 'European Council' when it brings
together the Heads of State or Government,
usually every quarter.

FIGURE 1 - THE INSTITUTIONAL TRIANGLE

II. COUNCIL OF THE EUROPEAN UNION

A. GENERAL DESCRIPTION

1. KEY QUESTIONS

WHAT IS IT?

The Council is probably the least well known of the three institutions, as most of its work is not public, and it tends to not be very transparent in its handlings. It brings together the government representatives of the Member States of the European Union (EU), at ministerial level (normal Council with different Ministers attending depending on the policy subject and meeting on a regular basis) or at head-of-state or government level (European Council, meeting usually every quarter, but with more meetings since 2010 due to the Euro financial crisis). It reflects the national interests and views of each Member State within the EU.

The Council is relevant at two levels:

- It is one of the key institutions involved in the decision-making process; and,

- The Permanent Representatives (the so-called "Perm Reps") or their attachés often provide guidance to the Members of the Parliament (MEPs) of their respective country (or at the very least to the MEPs of the political party of their government) regarding amendments to put forward and how to vote on a given legislative text.

WHERE IS IT?

The Council has its seat in Brussels, mainly in the Justus Lipsius Building -just opposite the Berlaymont Building where all the Commissioners have their offices – but also in a variety of rented buildings spread over Brussels (including the Kortenberg, Froissart, Espace Rolin, Woluwé Heights, Lex and Residence Palace Buildings). In April, June and October the Council holds its meetings at the Kirchberg Conference Centre in neighbouring Luxembourg. Finally, the Council is also allowed under exceptional circumstances and for duly justified reasons, to gather elsewhere than in Brussels or Luxembourg.

The Council is the main decision-making body of the European Union, notably as regards:

- The adoption of laws (often in cooperation with Parliament)[3];
- The coordination of economic policies across Europe;
- The definition and implementation of the EU's Common Foreign and Security Policy (CFSP);
- The conclusion of international agreements;
- The adoption of measures in the area of police and judicial cooperation in criminal matters; and,
- The adoption of the Community's annual budget (which hovers around €115 billion), in conjunction with Parliament.

The Council can issue a variety of acts to fulfil these tasks, namely regulations, directives, decisions, common actions or common positions, recommendations, opinions, conclusions, declarations or resolutions. When adopting legislation, the Council generally acts upon a proposal by the European Commission and in cooperation with the European Parliament -which explains why they are commonly referred to as the "Institutional Triangle".

Each Council member is accountable to its respective national parliament, and obviously represents and defends the national interests of its Member State.

WHY WOULD IT CARE ABOUT YOUR ISSUE?

Put bluntly, the Council as a patchwork of national interests does not care about the needs or desires of individual groups. Lobbying therefore mostly happens at a national level, by addressing the relevant ministries or relevant national authorities of a particular Member State.

In practice, this means that there's little point in wasting your time trying to lobby a certain Member State on behalf of your client unless the latter is an established company in that country, and preferably providing for a reasonable level of employment!

Only in certain circumstances will Council members' interests extend to companies not present in their countries as such but that still have an impact on

---

[3] See page 100 et seq. detailing the co-decision procedure.

them. This is notably the case for global Internet companies, which may not be established in every Member State but provide services or content accessible across the globe. A Voice over Internet provider or Google will for example ring a bell with any Council member, even if they are not established in their country.

FACTS & STATS

The Council of the European Union is also referred to as the "Council of Ministers", the "Council" or "Consilium". It is made up of:

- 2,300 officials within the Permanent Representations;

- 3,000 more coming regularly to Brussels as ad hoc national experts; and,

- 4,000 official servants working as permanent staff for the Council.

Note that the Council of the European Union should not be confused with the Council of Europe, the oldest international European level organisation (dating back to 1949) composed of 47 states and based in Strasbourg, France.

2. COUNCIL PRESIDENCIES

Why a plural, you may wonder. Isn't there just one permanent Council President since the entry into force of the Lisbon Treaty on 1 December 2009? Well, not exactly. Things are rarely simple at EU level, as outlined below.

PERMANENT PRESIDENT OF THE EUROPEAN COUNCIL

Since the entry into force of the Lisbon Treaty on 1 December 2009, the European Council has a permanent President, elected for two years and a half (renewable once) by a qualified majority (though the first President, Herman Van Rompuy, was appointed unanimously).

The President of the European Council mainly has two tasks:

- The representation of the Union, that now has its own legal personality under the Lisbon Treaty; and

- The chairing and coordination of the European Council.

So basically, the President sets the agenda (in close collaboration with the Secretary-General of the Council, whose role should not be underestimated), brokers deals, gives feedback to the other institutions and shakes hands.

The appointment of the Permanent President and the fact that the European Council now is a formally recognised institution have also rendered actual physical meetings of the European Council more regular, approximately every two months (except if a special meeting is required).

FACTS & STATS

Herman Van Rompuy, the Belgian former Prime Minister appointed as first President of the European Council, has the nickname 'Haiku Herman', due to his known passion for this Japanese form of poetry. He published a book with his own poems in 2010[4].

MEMBER STATES' ROTATING PRESIDENCIES & THE HIGH REPRESENTATIVE'S ROLE

Contrary to what some think, the appointment of a Permanent President has not put an end to the system of rotating presidencies, under which the Presidency of the Council is held in rotation every 6 months by a different Member State, in accordance with a pre-defined order set in a Council Decision.

The country holding the rotating Presidency plays an important role in organising the work of these Council configurations, both in terms of their political agenda and in terms of advancing legislative procedures, so it still is a lobbying target.

FACTS & STATS

The rotating presidencies from 2011 onwards are:

- Jan-Jun 2011:Hungary
- Jul-Dec 2011: Poland

---

[4] Herman Van Rompuy, 'Haiku', 2010.

- Jan-Jun 2012: Denmark
- Jul-Dec 2012: Cyprus
- Jan-Jun 2013: Ireland
- Jul-Dec 2013: Lithuania
- Jan-Jun 2014: Greece
- Jul-Dec 2014: Italy
- Jan-Jun 2015: Latvia
- Jul-Dec 2015: Luxembourg
- Jan-Jun 2016: Netherlands
- Jul-Dec 2016: Slovakia
- Jan-Jun 2017: Malta
- Jul-Dec 2017: United Kingdom
- Jan-Jun 2018: Estonia
- Jul-Dec 2018: Bulgaria
- Jan-Jun 2019: Austria
- Jul-Dec 2019: Romania
- Jan-Jun 2020: Finland

(1) WHO CHAIRS WHAT?

Under Article 16 paragraph 9 of the Lisbon Treaty, Member States will continue to chair most of the Council configurations[5], except for the Foreign Affairs Council, which is chaired by the High Representative[6], and the European Council (heads of State and Government), which is chaired by the permanent President.

The same combination will apply to the Committee of Permanent Representatives (referred to as Coreper[7]) chairmanship, although some documents indicate that as regards foreign affairs preparatory bodies, a split will exist between those chaired by the rotating presidency and those chaired by a member of the High Representative's team.

---

[5] See page 18 et seq. that detail how the Council works.
[6] See page 33 for more details on the High Representative.
[7] See page 21 for details on Coreper.

In other words, the chairmanships of meetings will be as follows:

- European Council: chaired by Permanent President;
- Foreign Affairs Council: chaired by the High Representative; and
- Eurogroup (initially an informal monthly meeting of Economy and Finance Ministers from the Euro-zone, which received a formal status through the Lisbon Treaty): chaired by the Eurogroup Chairman, appointed separately by the Council members for a two and a half year term.

(II) THE 'TROIKA' OR 'TRIO' CONCEPT

Since 2007, each of the rotating Presidencies works in "troika", i.e. in close cooperation as a "Trio of Presidencies", with the preceding , current and next Presidency, to ensure a certain level of coherence and planning over 18 months, rather than just 6 months. In the past, due to the fact that each 6-month Presidency worked on a stand-alone basis, they were referred to in Brussels 'stop-start' Presidencies. The troika coherence is ensured by the fact that the trio of presidencies must present their joint programme (prepared in collaboration with the European Commission) to the General Affairs Council at least one month before the 18-month period starts.

The resources burden of such a Presidency can be impressive, when one considers that the presiding country organises an average of 3500 meetings over a six-month period (even though this is expected to slightly decrease with the Permanent President and High Representative roles).

SURVIVAL TIP

In general, Member States in charge of a Presidency must assume a more neutral role, as they chair the meeting of the working groups, Corepers and Councils. This can mean that, as a lobbyist, you lose an important ally in the Member State that holds the Presidency, as its representatives will be much more reluctant to introduce your amendments or changes at their own initiative.

They can however still play a crucial role as a source of information and in the way they conduct discussions and use procedural rules to either speed up the adoption of a legislative measure or delay it.

3.   PERMANENT REPRESENTATIONS

Permanent Representations play a key role in ensuring the day-to-day follow-up of all matters handled at Council levels: they supply information and analysis to their respective national government on everything that happens at EU level and more specifically within the Council and transmit their government's positions and viewpoints to the relevant EU institutions.

Their main task is to act as an 'extended arm' of their national government in Brussels and to ensure that the interests and policies of their country are pursued as effectively as possible within the EU.

Permanent Representations are headed by a Permanent Representative who carries the title of Ambassador and is assisted by a Deputy. Both play an active role through their presence in the Committee of Permanent Representatives (Coreper), the body responsible for preparing the political aspect of the files (or "dossiers") discussed at Council.

Many of the civil servants working in the Permanent Representations have actually been assigned to their respective post by various national ministries. Job titles vary from First Secretary, Counsellor, Attaché, and so on, not taking into account the military staff working in each Permanent Representation.

In many cases, although the decision-making power lies very much at the national level in terms of the Council (in other words, it is more effective to lobby directly at the level of the national ministries), the staff of the Permanent Representations are worth meeting as they sit in most of the Working Groups (that prepare all the technical legislative work submitted to the Ambassadors and the Council Ministers[8]) and are more likely to pay attention to an issue for which they received some detailed explanation by stakeholders.

---

[8] See page 23.

THE PERM REP CLUB

I have often been told that the Council needs to be influenced at national level, in the capital cities of each Member State. In many cases, it is certainly accurate to say that the national ministries in charge of a specific portfolio usually carry the biggest weight when it comes to specifying the political priorities and direction a dossier will take.

But don't be too quick to dismiss the influence of the Permanent representations based in Brussels. These are the diplomatic missions of each Member State to the EU and the "bubble" nature of Brussels politics reflects itself in this "Little Club" formed by the Perm reps, Deputy Perm reps, antici, attachés, etc. based in Brussels.

I once had the honour of giving a speech at a panel discussion organised in the European Parliament at which that "club" effect was physically visible in the room: to the left of the room, there was a cluster of lobbyists representing the rights holder interests; to the right were the representatives of large telecoms companies. At first, the attachés from the permanent representations trickled separately into the room and sat randomly. But as soon as the session stopped for a short break, everyone assembled immediately in the back of the room, like members of a university fraternity (beer kegs excluded, obviously).

The influence of these young attachés should therefore not be underestimated. They often play an important role in shaping the opinion of their national government and ambassador, especially regarding issues that are less present in the public eye. When a Minister needs to make last-minute decisions, a recommendation whispered at that moment by an attaché can tip the balance in one direction or another.

Rotating presidencies of Member States are perfectly aware of this fact, and some try to bypass the technical expertise of attachés by trying to push discussions immediately at Permanent Representative level where discussions are less about the specifics of a dossier and more of political considerations. This usually vastly annoys the attachés, as it creates decisions based on political motivations alone, but without the required technical input.

Finally, the importance of these attachés is also mirrored by the fact that they are increasingly asked by industry stakeholders to join their company as lobbyists –

sometimes under rather dubious circumstances. I lobbied not so long ago on a piece of legislation that went through a full co-decision procedure during two years (and hence four different Council presidencies). During that time, two of the three attachés leading for their respective presidency the negotiations relating to that dossier, were hired only a couple of weeks after the end of that presidency (and hence still under the "troika" period) by major companies that had heavily lobbied that dossier. As a government representative told me at that time, it makes one wonder if Ministries should not pay more attention to due process and the rules of common sense, and set in place revolving door prohibitions under certain circumstances, even for non senior personnel.

B.   How the Council Works

1.   Per subject: Council Formations

Councils are organised according to ten different configurations that basically reflect the broad themes handled at EU level. They are generally referred to by their unpronounceable acronyms, some of which come from their French name:

- General Affairs (Genaff), which prepares European Councils and handles issues covering various Council formations;
- Foreign Affairs (Foraff), which covers development cooperation as well as the Common Foreign and Security Policy (CFSP) including the Common Security and Defence Policy (CSDP);
- Economic and Financial Affairs (Ecofin), which also covers budget;
- Agriculture and Fisheries;
- Employment, Social Policy, Health and Consumer Affairs (EPSCO);
- Justice and Home Affairs (JHA), including civil protection;
- Competitiveness (Comp), which covers Internal Market, Industry and Research, including tourism;
- Transport, Telecommunications and Energy (TTE);
- Environment (ENVI); and,
- Education, Youth and Culture (EYC), which also covers audiovisual affairs.

'Jumbo' Councils happen when different Council configurations meet at the same time to discuss transversal issues.

The Ministers attending Council meetings will obviously vary according to the configuration. Also, in certain cases of split portfolio, more than one minister will represent a Member State at a Council meeting (for example if different Ministers are in charge of Telecoms and Energy for a given Member State, both will attend a TTE Council if there are relevant matters to them on the agenda).

The General Affairs, Foreign Affairs, Ecofin and Agriculture and Fisheries Councils meet every month, while other configurations tend to be more irregular.

2. PREPARATORY WORK: GENERAL SECRETARIAT, WORKING GROUPS AND COREPER

	SENSITIVE ISSUES* (political, institutional, economic)	TECHNICAL ISSUES*
*List of examples is not exhaustive		
Working Parties (WP) (permanent or ad hoc) **WHAT?** Preparatory work or studies, e.g. in relation to amendments proposed by the EP in co-decision. **WHO?** Representatives of the Member States (usually experts from the national ministries or relevant regulatory authorities), as well as attachés or advisers from each Permanent Representation.	-WP on General Affairs -WP of Foreign Relations Counsellors -WP on Financial Questions	-High Level WG on Agriculture -WP on Competitiveness and Growth -WP on Social Questions
Committees **WHAT?** Preparatory work for the Council. **WHO?** Representatives of the Member States (usually experts from the national ministries or relevant regulatory authorities), as well as attachés or advisers from each Permanent Representation.	-Economic and Financial Committee -Economic Policy Committee -Policy and Security Committee Military Committee -Strategic Committee on Immigration, Frontiers and Asylum -Trade Policy Committee	-Special Committee on Agriculture -Employment Committee -Social Protection Committee -Education Committee -Committee on Cultural Affairs
Coordination Groups **WHAT?** Coordination of the different Committees and Working Groups. **WHO?** Representatives of the Member States (Counsellors) specifically assigned to this task.	- Antici Group	- Mertens Group
Coreper **WHAT?** Preparing the work and carrying out the tasks assigned by the Council. **WHO?** Permanent Representatives and Deputy Permanent Representatives.	- Coreper II	- Coreper I
Council **WHAT?** Decisions. **WHO?** Representatives of the Member States at Ministerial level.	-General Affairs -Foreign Affairs -Economic and Financial Affairs -Justice and Home Affairs	-Agriculture and Fisheries -Competitiveness -Employment, Social Policy, Health and Consumer Affairs -Transport, Telecoms and Energy

FIGURE 2 – HOW WORK IS PREPARED AT THE COUNCIL

In practice, once a proposal for a decision from the Commission has been put before the Council, specialist working groups and committees begin to prepare the Council's position. There are at present over 150 such specialised bodies.

The work carried out in these preparatory bodies, with the assistance of the General Secretariat of the Council, is then submitted to the Committee of Permanent Representatives (or 'Coreper'[9]), bringing together the "EU Ambassadors" and their deputies. Coreper normally reviews each single item on the agenda ahead of every Council meeting, and in quite a few cases comes to an agreement that simply needs to be approved without discussion by the Council. This filtering of issues allows the Council to focus mainly on the political issues, the technical matters having been solved upstream.

GENERAL SECRETARIAT OF THE COUNCIL

The General Secretariat of the Council (or 'Council Secretariat') is made up of roughly 4000 civil servants that assist the Council and its Presidency in multiple ways.

From an organisational viewpoint, the Secretariat ensures that the various meetings are properly prepared; assists in the drafting of reports (including legal advice); and is in charge of the handling of translations, records, documents, agendas and general presidency-related tasks. This is done for the working parties, as well as for the Coreper, Council of Ministers and European Council.

In addition, the Secretariat acts as an honest broker and provides legal advice at the EU's Intergovernmental Conferences (IGC).

Headed by the Secretary General of the EU, the General Secretariat also comprises a legal service, eight directorates-general (named alphabetically from A to I) and a private office offering support to the Secretary-General and his Deputy.

SURVIVAL TIP

The Secretariat tends to play a more important role when smaller Member States hold the rotating Presidency (as they have less resources), especially when the Member State in question is in charge of a Presidency for the first time - as was recently the case for several 'new' Member States such as Slovenia or the Czech Republic, which relied more heavily on the Secretariat than the 'older' Member States (e.g. Germany, France, etc.) usually do.

---

[9] See page 21.

The Committee of Permanent Representatives (Coreper, from the French *Comité des représentants permanents*) ensures that Member States have a permanent presence at the European Union's headquarters. It also enables the Council to focus on major political issues at their meetings, most of the other issues having been prepared and dealt with at Coreper level.

Theoretically Coreper can only issue non-binding guidelines to the Council, but practice proves that the Council will generally confirm the agreements reached by Coreper. In fact, an estimated 80 to 90 percent of Council decisions have been struck at Coreper level!

Coreper is divided into two configurations, which each meet at least once a week:

- Coreper part 1 or 'Coreper I' brings together the Deputy Permanent Representatives and deals with more technical matters (e.g. employment, competitiveness, transport, telecommunications, energy, agriculture, environment, education). Coreper I meets on Wednesdays and occasionally on Fridays as well.

- Coreper part 2 or 'Coreper II' brings together the Permanent Representatives (that generally hold the rank of Ambassador extraordinary and plenipotentiary and are commonly referred to as the "perm reps") and deals with politically sensitive areas or institutional and general issues (e.g. General Affairs, Ecofin, Justice and Home Affairs). Coreper II meets normally on Thursdays, except in the weeks preceding the meetings of the Council for General Affairs and the Ecofin Council. In that case, the meeting is held on Wednesdays.

As a consequence of these weekly meetings, attachés preparing the briefings are nearly always on the edge, Thursday afternoon and Friday being often the best days to meet with them.

In both Corepers, the Permanent Representatives and their deputies act on instructions from their national authorities.

Each configuration tries to reach an agreement on decisions before submitting them to the Council. If they have achieved consensus, the Council generally adopts it as an 'A point', also known as approval without debate. If certain issues have not been solved through Coreper negotiations, the item appears as a 'B point' on the agenda and is subject to debate. Finally, in some cases, items appear as 'fake B points', when the Council wants to show an item is too important not to be debated, but at the same time, the debate is purely formal as the deal has been closed before.

Before becoming 'A' or 'B' points at Council, items are similarly split into Part I and Part II agenda points at Coreper meetings. Part I items have been agreed on in the Council working groups and are generally (but not necessarily) approved without debate, whilst items under Part II must be examined. Moreover, when looking at a Coreper agenda, one can see sometimes see items marked "as the case may be": these can be deleted by the chair at short notice. In some cases, a lobbyist trying to buy some time will try to convince a permanent representation (or more) to push an item on the 'B' or Part II list of agenda points, to ensure more debate is necessary before reaching an agreement (time which the lobbyist could need to push their proposal forward).

Coreper must also carry out any task assigned by the Council. Usually these requests are related to the further study of a dossier or a report on a specific issue.

COMMITTEES

Usually committees can only be set up by Council or Coreper, or with the explicit approval of one of them. However a number of Special Committees were set up by Treaties to coordinate the Council's activities in particular areas, while the Special Committee on Agriculture (SCA) was specifically set up by the European Council in 1960.

These so-called 'High-level Committees' include:

- Economic and Financial Committee;
- Trade Policy Committee (formerly referred to as Committee 133), dealing with tariffs and trade in the area of the Common Trade Policy;
- Political and Security Committee;
- Article 36 Coordinating Committee, dealing with the area of police and judicial cooperation in criminal matters;
- Economic Policy Committee;
- European Union Military Committee (EUMC); and,
- Special Committee on Agriculture (SCA).

Working Groups can only be set up by Council or Coreper, or with the approval of one of them. They are split into ad hoc groups that have a limited time span, and so-called standing groups which deal with specific sectors on an ongoing basis.

A special set of horizontal Working Groups responsible for preparing Coreper meetings are the Antici Group (Coreper II), the Mertens Group (Coreper I) and the Friends of the Presidency Group (ad hoc body studying the multidisciplinary aspects of specific issues).

The Mertens and Antici Groups, made up respectively of the personal assistants of Coreper I and Coreper II members, meet the day before the actual Coreper meetings. With the help of the General Secretariat Cabinet and a member of the Legal Service, they finalise the order of the Coreper agenda, items that can be raised under "any other business", and the final list of reservations expressed by Member States on specific documents. In other words, a lot of the ground work is done by the representatives attending these meetings, who carry quite a bit of weight in the decision-making process.

3.   COUNCIL VOTING MECHANISM

Theoretically, the Council votes by simple majority, qualified majority or unanimity, depending on the subject matter and/or the legislative procedural stage at which a vote is cast.

But in practice, voting procedures are not that important as most files are handled and agreed on at the lower levels and Council tries to reach most of its decisions by consensus, without a formal vote (voting rules being merely used as a pressure tool to reach compromises that avoid qualified majority voting).

With the entry into force of the Lisbon Treaty, qualified majority votes ('QMV') have become the rule as many areas previously requiring unanimity are now voted by QMV (e.g. external border control, asylum, immigration, etc.).

The calculation rules to obtain this QMV are quite complex and will vary in time due to changes brought about by the Lisbon Treaty and the adoption of various transitional measures.

Though the Lisbon Treaty has been adopted and changes the voting rules, these changes will only apply from 31 October 2014, meaning that the system currently in place is still the one provided by the Nice Treaty of 2001. Under this system, each Member State has a certain number of votes depending on its size (the biggest states having 29 votes, whilst the smallest ones only have 3) and 255 votes (out of a total of 345) are necessary for a decision to be adopted.

From 31 October 2014 onwards, a decision adopted under QMV requires a double majority:

- The votes must represent 55%[10] of <u>EU Member States</u> (i.e. at 27, 15 Member States); and,
- The votes must represent 65% of the <u>EU's population</u>.

There is however a transitional period whereby between 1 November 2014 and March 2017, any Member State may request that the current weighted voting system be applied instead of the new double majority system.

THE CONCEPT OF 'BLOCKING MINORITY'

The transitional rules until 31 October 2014 also apply to the 'blocking minority' concept. Under the current rules, Member States representing 35 percent of the EU's population can block a legislative measure.

Under the Lisbon Treaty, from 2014 onwards, at least four Member States representing at least 35 percent of the EU population will be needed for a blocking minority. This is going to significantly reduce the possibility to block legislation compared to the pre-Lisbon Treaty system, which only required a combination of three of the biggest EU Member States (easily representing the needed 35 percent).

---

[10] This percentage applies to all cases where the Council votes on a European Commission proposal. In the exceptional cases where the Council acts on its own initiative, 72 percent of Member States must be represented.

SURVIVAL TIP

Blocking minorities can be an interesting tool in certain cases. In one case, the fact that I informed very thoroughly all smaller Member States that a specific Decision the Commission was trying to push forward would imply that their country would not benefit from a satellite service, created a blocking minority threat which was sufficient to ensure the final text of the Decision was more balanced than the Commission's initial proposal. This required three vocal small Member States getting the support of one larger one (i.e. Poland), the rest of the smaller ones than following suit. This did not make me very popular with the Commission department in charge of this file but served my client well.

THE 'IONNINA COMPROMISE' IN THE EVENT OF A NARROW QMV MAJORITY

For controversial dossiers where obtaining a QMV is difficult, Poland required the adoption of a transitional rule - the so-called Ionnina Compromise[11] - to ratify the Lisbon Treaty.

Under this transitional rule, a small number of countries can force the Council to continue discussing an act even if they do not have a proper blocking minority and a qualified majority was reached. To make this request, at least one of two criteria must be met:

- 75% of the number of Member States necessary for the formation of a blocking minority – blocking minorities requiring 3 Member states at present; or,
- 75% of the population necessary for the formation of a blocking minority.

These numbers imply that the reached QMV is very narrow.

Under such an exceptional scenario, Council must try to reach a broader agreement. However, this process cannot, however, happen to the detriment of any of the deadlines set in place by the Treaty or by other rules. It can therefore not be compared to an indefinite veto power.

---

[11] Named after the Greek town where the Foreign Affairs Ministers struck a deal in 1994 which inspired this measure.

III. European Commission

A. General Description

1. What is it?

The term 'Commission' refers both to the College of Commissioners (i.e. the heads of the Commission appointed by each Member State and approved by the European Parliament) and to the actual institution and its more than 25,000 civil servants.

Together with the Council and the European Parliament, the Commission is the executive arm responsible for implementing EU laws, the legislative arm or initiator of such laws and the 'Guardian of the Treaties'.

The Commission is supposed to reason and act in the interest of the EU, regardless of the nationality of the Commissioner leading on a given dossier. In practice however, national pressures have been exerted on Commissioners, and it is difficult to tell to what extent such pressures are effective or not. Former Competition Commissioner Van Miert[12] once told me at a dinner that the biggest challenge facing the Commission now (as compared to the early days of the institution) was the fact that the appointed Commissioners were still young and ambitious enough to hope going back to their home country to make a national political career. From his point of view, this meant that national pressure was more likely to have an influence than back in the days when becoming a Commissioner was an 'end of career' move.

---

[12] European Commissioner from 1989 to 1999, first in charge of Transport (1989-1993), then of Competition (1993-1999). Deceased in 2009.

FACTS & STATS

To summarise the European Commission in a few figures:

- 27 Commissioners each with their own Cabinet;
- About 25,000 civil servants (many of them being translators and interpreters);
- 40 Directorates-General plus a series of services (legal services, translation, etc.); and
- 36 Agencies spread across Europe.

2. WHERE IS IT?

The seat of the Commission is in Brussels, Belgium but it also has offices in Luxembourg, as well as 'representation' offices in every Member State and 'delegations' outside the EU.

3. WHAT DOES IT DO?

The European Commission has four main roles:

- Propose legislation to the Parliament and the Council through its right of initiative. It does so after consulting stakeholders and requesting the advice of the European Economic and Social Committee (ESC) and the Committee of the Regions (CoR), and in most cases, also the opinions of national parliaments and governments. Its scope of action is mainly limited by the so-called principle of subsidiarity, whereby the Commission should only intervene when, and to the extent that, an issue cannot be handled at national or local level;
- Manage and implement EU policies and the budget as the EU's executive arm. The Commission needs to get discharge for implementing the budget by the European Parliament, which looks closely at the opinion issued by the Court of Auditors and tends to use its budgetary power to exert political pressure;
- Enforce European law (jointly with the Court of Justice), as Guardian of the Treaties. This practically means that the Commission can launch an infringement proceeding against a Member State, first through the sending of an official letter to the concerned government, then through a court case

before the European Court of Justice (ECJ) if a Member State fails to implement or improperly transposes EU legislation into national law. Decisions by the ECJ are binding and can include penalties; and,

- <u>Represent the European Union on the international stage</u>, for example by negotiating agreements between the EU and other countries. It does notably so at the World Trade Organisation (WTO) and in bilateral trade agreements.

SURVIVAL TIP

For a lobbyist, the European Commission is usually the first port of call to either lobby an issue that is on the agenda, or bring a new issue to the Commission's attention to motivate them into action - either by including an issue in a planned initiative or, more rarely, by convincing the officials to add a new item on their list of deliverables.

---

4. WHY WOULD IT CARE?

The European Commission is an interesting mixture of political thinking (mostly at Commissioner and Cabinet levels) and a bureaucratic and technical approach (at Directorate-General level).

Getting both levels to care can be achieved in different manners.

From a technical point of view, providing them with well-argued documents early on can help shape their thinking process by providing sufficiently balanced arguments. Do not hesitate to involve your engineers or chemists or any other technical staff that can help the person handling the dossier within the Commission to better understand all the layers and subtleties it comprises.

Moreover, getting involved early on will also help disarm the Commission staff's common complaint of "Why did you not come to us before with this issue?", referring generally to a Green Paper or other form of consultation issued previously. Basically, do not give them an excuse to say: "We did not realise...".

Finally, feeding your arguments and ideas to a civil servant at an early stage often means (1) they could be grateful and rely on you as a source to reflect ideas on and (2) your point of view will be integrated in the Commission's document as its own.

At a political level, every Commissioner is different and therefore making them care is dependent on their nature. Some are media-hungry and keen on constructing a specific public image in the press (the defender of the little people, the intransigent upholder of competition, etc). Some display a strong national concern, while others come from a background that pushes them to focus more on certain issues. Each of them also has a political colour (left or right wing) which affects the way they look at things. In addition, the level of influence cabinets exert on their Commissioner, and the number of individuals in control of that influence within the Cabinet can also vary quite a bit: it is not always the Head of Cabinet that runs the show!

ASSOCIATIONS, GRASSROOTS Vs ASTROTURF AND THE BRAND NEW EUROPEAN CITIZENS' INITIATIVE PRINCIPLE

The European Commission tends to listen more to associations than to individual industry players. Hence conveying one's message at association level can be more effective.

But this also has a perverse effect: companies now create shell associations which supposedly represent the joint interests of different entities, but in reality are used as a vehicle to 'make the numbers' for a specific agenda. These empty shell organisations are usually easy to spot thanks to certain hints:

- A nominal membership fee. The famous saying "There is no such thing as a free lunch" holds, like most proverbs, a lot of truth. If an association has few members, it is especially odd that a small fee would be required to join;
- A multi-event organisation (panel discussions, European Parliament breakfasts, etc) with either a single sponsor or no identifiable sponsor; and,
- A focus on 'enemy bashing', be it a competitor to the interests hiding behind the association, a specific institution, value, etc.

In parallel to this phenomenon, Brussels has also been the target of both grassroots and so-called astroturf campaigns. A lot has been written to differentiate these two types of movements, based on their spontaneous Vs orchestrated origin, funding, motivation, etc. To me, any campaign created by a set of informed individuals who strive to inspire citizens to communicate a concern or voice support for a specific legislation or equivalent project, merits the name "grassroots", regardless of whether its founders are a bunch of mates down the local pub, an NGO or a multi-national corporation.

Astroturf, on the other hand, applies to imposters: spam emails from fake organisations which conceal a group of people trying to mislead decision-makers into thinking there is a "broad concern" about a certain issue. They generally also provide misleading or false information to citizens in order to convince them to support a dubious cause.

The distinction between both approaches will be extremely important in the future, with the inclusion of the 'European Citizens' Initiative' (ECI)[13] in the EU legislative framework by the Lisbon Treaty. This new tool aimed at increasing direct democracy enables one million EU citizens, who are nationals of a significant number of Member States, to call directly on the European Commission to bring forward an initiative of interest to them in an area of EU competence. The specifics on how such an initiative would be deemed acceptable need to be set out in a Regulation, which is currently still under discussion. The guiding principles under the Lisbon Treaty are that the initiative should not be "foolish" and concern something that falls under the scope of the EU legislator, and that 1 million citizens of a "significant number of Member States" must sign the relevant petition.

Additional details should be agreed on at the start of 2011 (e.g. time limit for the collection of signatures, minimum age of signatories, etc.), with the Commission having put forward a draft Regulation which is currently being examined by the other institutions. It is to be expected that grassroots and astroturf campaigns will become even more prominent features of EU lobbying.

---

[13] Art. 11, Par. 4 of the Treaty on European Union (TEU) and Art. 24, Par. 1 of the Treaty on the Functioning of the European Union (TFEU).

B.   Commissioners and their Staff

1.   Commissioners

Role

Though put forward by their national government, members of the Commission (or 'Commissioners' as they are informally referred to) are supposed to act in the interest of the EU as a whole, and not be influenced by their national governments or interests.

From a more personal perspective, however, their culture and the fact that most of them are former national politicians who return home at the end of their term, is likely to have some partisan impact on their action.

Appointment Procedure

Commissioners are appointed every five years, within six months of the European Parliament elections.

First, the President of the Commission is designated jointly by the Member States and approved by Parliament. Then, Member States put forward their candidate Commissioner in discussion with the President of the Commission; the Council adopts that list by qualified majority and submits the candidates to the questions and vote of Parliament. Under the Lisbon Treaty, the European Parliament's approval occurs in two phases: first, the Parliament must approve the President of the Commission, and then it gets to approve the Commission as a body. This procedure is preceded by public hearings, where each Commissioner-designate has to answer to a series of questions from the MEPs of the parliamentary committee(s) responsible for their portfolio during a three-hour session. Council then enacts this vote, again by qualified majority.

In terms of each Commissioner's portfolio, a fair bit of horse trading occurs but on paper, the President of the Commission allocates responsibilities, and reshuffles them if required. The President can also force a Commissioner to resign, provided all other Commissioners approve. The entire Commission can also be dismissed by the European Parliament, through the adoption of a motion of censure, referred to as 'the nuclear option'.

The High Representative for Common Foreign and Security Policy

While the role of High Representative (often inaccurately referred to as the 'Foreign Affairs Minister') has existed for some time now, its scope and status have been considerably expanded by the Lisbon Treaty. The High Representative is now:

- A Vice-President of the Commission;
- The chair of the Council of Foreign Affairs Ministers and acts as a spokesperson on foreign policy in those areas where the EU is able to reach an agreement;
- In charge of both the Common Foreign and Security Policy (CFSP) and External Relations (previously two separate portfolios) supported by a 'diplomacy corps' called the European External Action Service (EEAS); and,
- One of the Commissioners (with the President) taking part in the work of the European Council.

The High Representative is appointed by the European Council, with the agreement of the President of the Commission and by a qualified majority vote.

Meetings & Interactions

The Commissioners usually meet every week on Wednesday in Brussels (except during the plenary weeks of the European Parliament in Strasbourg, when Commissioners also meet in Strasbourg on Tuesday), on the 13th floor of the Berlaymont building.

Each Commissioner presents the dossiers relevant to their portfolio and all the others decide jointly on it, in 'collegial' manner (expression referring to the "College of Commissioners" and implying the Commission decides collectively, not individually).[14]

The agenda is prepared by the Secretariat-General and handed to the Commissioners one day before the meeting. The agenda and minutes of these meetings can be accessed at the Register of Commission Documents.

---

[14] For more details, see page 90 that details the Inter-service consultation mechanism.

Under the Lisbon Treaty, the number of Commissioners will gradually be reduced:

The 2010-2014 Commission has one Commissioner per Member State (i.e. 27 in total, including the President), with several of these Commissioners also carrying the hat of 'Vice-President'. Among them is the High Representative for Foreign Affairs and Security Policy.

From 2014 onwards, the number of Commissioners should correspond to two-thirds of the Member States. Commissioners will be appointed by rotation, with care being taken to ensure that countries are represented fairly, taking into account the demographic and geographical range of all the Member States (i.e. a mix of small and large countries, western and eastern European ones, north and south, etc.). It remains however to be seen if this will work in practice.

2.   CABINETS

ROLE

Cabinets are extremely powerful and are there to give political guidance to their Commissioner (as opposed to the technical guidance given by the Directorates-General).

SURVIVAL TIP

For a lobbyist, selling an argument to the Cabinet member leading on a dossier or, even better, the Head of Cabinet, is more than half of the job when trying to obtain the Commissioner's support. Some issues will even be agreed on amongst the Heads of Cabinet, without ever being raised to the Commissioner's attention.

COMPOSITION

The composition of Cabinets is theoretically restricted by a number of more or less explicit rules:

- There can only be six cabinet members;
- At least two cabinet members must be women;
- A maximum of three members can be of the same nationality as the Commissioner; and,
- The composition must reflect the European Union's regional diversity.

The Head of Cabinet is called under his French denomination, *Chef de Cabinet* (pronounced 'cab-i-nay') or '*Chef de cab*".

MEETINGS & INTERACTIONS

The Cabinets of all Commissioners interact in various ways to prepare the weekly meetings of their Commissioners. The most important configurations are:

- The <u>Hebdo</u>: at this set weekly meeting ('hebdo' being short for the French word '*hebdomadaire*' meaning weekly), all heads of cabinet discuss day-to-day dossiers and ensure their content is adequately prepared prior to the Commissioners' meetings; and,

- The <u>Special Chefs</u>: these are ad hoc meetings set up between the relevant members of each cabinet for a specific area, the legal service and the secretariat general, to discuss last-minute compromises to draft legislation before it gets discussed at the College of Commissioners. Note that a lot of preparation happens in corridors and many deals are often struck between cabinets outside the meeting rooms. In this case, the cabinet of the President tends to play a 'broker's' role. One of the most important special chefs is the Group for Inter-Institutional Relations, which analyses the European Parliament's views on Commission-proposed legislation in order to prepare the Commission for an eventual rejection.

3.   DIRECTORATES-GENERAL

The nearly 25,000 civil servants, who take care of the Commission's day-to-day running, are spread across some 40 departments known as Directorates-General (DGs), and various other services (e.g. translation, publications, legal service, etc.).

Each DG covers a specific policy area or service, and is headed by a Director-General who reports to a Commissioner. Each DG is subdivided into directorates and each directorate is in turn subdivided into units.

The DGs are at the heart of the drafting process but their work needs to be approved by their Commissioner first (and this often means their Cabinet), followed by the Legal Service and the Secretariat-General, and then undergo an inter-service consultation in order to be approved by the College of Commissioners at one of their Wednesday meetings, by at least 14 votes out of 27.

All the DGs and services are coordinated by the Secretariat-General, headed by a Secretary-General that reports directly to the President.

IV.   European Parliament

A.   Description

1.   What is it?

The European Parliament (EP) presents itself as "the Voice of the People", seeing that it is the only EU institution directly elected by citizens (since 1979).

The EP is elected for five years (although the term of certain MEPs can be shorter depending on their country's national rules of designation or if they decide to go back to national politics during their term) and every EU citizen is entitled to vote and to stand as candidate in any Member state.

There are currently 736 MEPs. This number should go up to 751 in 2014 (and 754 between end of 2010 and 2014[15]), as the rules of the Lisbon Treaty will apply to the 2014 European elections.

2.   Where is it?

The European Parliament is officially seated in Strasbourg, France, even though MEPs are only there one week per month, for the plenary sessions.

The remaining three weeks are mostly spent in Brussels, notably for Committee and Political Group meetings.

The General-Secretariat, i.e. the administrative offices of the Parliament, is located in Luxembourg.

3.   What does it do?

The EP's work can be split into two phases: the preparation of the plenary sessions (where issues are discussed within specialised Committees and Political Groups meetings), and the plenary sessions themselves, during which the Parliament votes.

---

[15] This number should have increased temporarily to 754 MEPs after the adoption of the Lisbon Treaty, to then decrease again to 751 MEPs after the 2014 elections. However, procedural issues have so far not rendered it feasible to go from 736 MEPs (number set by the Treaty of Nice) to 754 MEPs. This has led to many commentators to criticise the so-called 18 Shadow MEPs who seem unable to start their work. These 18 MEPs should start their work in fall 2010, once Member States have signed a protocol to the Lisbon Treaty.

The EP's tasks are three-fold:

- The Parliament is <u>co-legislator</u> with the Council in many policy areas, even though the right of initiative in terms of legislation lies with the Commission;
- The Parliament holds a democratic <u>supervision</u> right over the EU institutions and in particular over the European Commission: it needs to approve each new Commission and Commissioner, and can revoke a Commission as a whole through a motion of censure; and,
- The Parliament, together with the Council, must approve the annual EU <u>budget</u>, which does not come into force until the President of the Parliament has signed it. The duo is also in charge of 'granting a discharge', i.e. of approving the way in which the budget is spent every year.

FACTS & STATS

To summarise the European Parliament in a few figures:

- Number of MEPs: 736 MEPs after 2009 elections (down from 785 in the 2004-2009 parliament) but with a transitional arrangement that allows for 754 MEPs until 2014, when the total number of MEPs will be the one set in the Lisbon Treaty, namely 751 MEPs (750 + president), with Germany's delegation being reduced from 99 MEPs to 96.
- Each MEP has one to three assistants split into seven political groups that each have their own staff;
- About 7,500 civil servants operate in 23 official languages. In the top five of represented nationalities, Belgium ranks first (955), followed by France (852), Italy (703), Germany (656) and Spain (503)[16];
- 20 Committees, 2 sub-Committees and 1 ad hoc Committee, all specialised in specific legislative areas; and,
- 36 delegations handling relations with national Parliaments across the world.

---

[16] Numbers collected in 2010.

B. MEMBERS OF THE EUROPEAN PARLIAMENT (MEPs)

1. WHO ARE THEY?

Many MEPs are former members of national parliaments (about 35%) or former ministers or equivalent (about 15%), at both senior and junior levels.

About one third (35%) of the MEPs are women, Malta (with no women), Luxemburg and the Czech Republic ranking lowest, and Finland (with 62%), Sweden and Estonia being the frontrunners[17].

Some MEPs are also the leaders of their national political party (mostly smaller parties); some are former Commissioners of the European Commission; and some have held important Regional Office Functions, while others are former or even serving mayors.

Finally, MEPs also include former judges, trade union leaders, media personalities as well as a number of doctors, lawyers and academics. And a few MEPs were actually former assistants to MEPs.

Since 2004, they are no longer allowed to hold a dual mandate (except for a few legacy cases in Ireland and the UK).

---

[17] Numbers collected in 2010.

THE FRENCH, GERMAN OR ITALIAN CONNECTION

Everyone in Brussels always talks about the German and the French connection - and no, people don't mean drug cartels when they whisper about this in the polished corridors of the Berlaymont building. But any nation can play an important role, as long as it is either big or vocal enough (or preferably both). Frequently, the power struggle is coloured by prejudice and stereotyping, which can prove rather bemusing to an outsider. The finest example I have ever encountered in practice occurred when I enquired why Polish MEPs were fighting so hard for an obscure amendment in a legislative discussion, and a French MEP's assistant replied with a twinkle in his eye: "Oh, I told them they would annoy the Germans by supporting this".

Now, I tend to think that sounds too easy (and basic) to be true. At a more real(istic) level, I have seen the interesting chemistry of national connections occur with the Italian contingent within the European Parliament. The best thing that can happen when you are a freelance lobbyist is having clients that appreciate the value of personality and cultural sensitivities (and believe me, that happens less often than you would think). It so happens that one of my clients truly understood this and had taken what I like to call the "full Monty"[18] approach to Brussels lobbying: on the one hand, they hired a technical lobbyist (me!) skilled at writing position papers and presenting well-argued cases to defend an amendment in front of specialist MEPs, MEP assistants, political advisors and Committee secretariats; and, on the other, they found a former politician able to open the door to all the MEPs of her country and trigger the necessary "goodwill" for those MEPs to listen to the arguments.

In practice, this knock-out combination meant that when I needed to table an amendment for my client at plenary session (which procedurally requires that the amendment be supported by 40 MEPs), I managed to obtain 19 signatures from the MEPs of one single country - not because my client's activities were of such high importance in that given country, but because the goodwill created by their peer politician friend had led one of the MEPs to bring the amendment to a lunch organised by his Prime Minister, and got all his colleagues to sign it between cheese and coffee!

---

[18] For anyone thinking that this chapter is now taking an odd direction, please note that the "full Monty" here should be understood under its definition "Everything which is necessary, appropriate, or possible; 'the works' and does not refer to the closing scenes of the homonymous 1997 movie.

2.   WHERE ARE THEY?

MEPs spend quite a substantial amount of their time travelling for work.

Their 'hang-outs' are:

- 1 week a month in Strasbourg France for plenary (weeks usually stretching from Tuesday to Thursday);
- Up to three weeks a month in Brussels in plenary session, Committee, and Political Group meetings (though the latter sometimes take place in more exotic locations);
- Occasionally in other countries, notably in the framework of their Delegations work[19]; and,
- And a couple of days a week (including weekends) in their home constituency.

3.   WHAT DO THEY DO?

IN GENERAL

(I) VOTING DISCIPLINE (OR LACK OF THEREOF...)

MEPs are either members of one of the seven Political Groups or 'non-attached' (i.e. independent from any European political group). But they are also members of their country delegation and this can lead to conflicting voting behaviour between the voting discipline as set by a Political Group as a whole and the voting discipline required by national interests!

Individual MEPs can help forge the voting discipline of their political party and some individual MEPs can play a substantial role as back-benchers.

(II) DIFFERENT FORMS OF INTERVENTION

MEPs can:

- Put questions to the Commission or Council, either at question time (oral procedure) or in view to obtain a written answer. But to be honest, given the poor attendance at many plenary sessions outside voting time, question

---

[19] See page 51.

time in plenary does not carry much impact. Written questions have the merit of putting things 'on the record';

- Table a motion for resolution or a written declaration. These rarely end up translating into a Committee Report, but do allow an MEP (sometimes inspired by a lobbyist) to create 'noise' around an issue;
- Table amendments to any text in committee;
- Explain a vote prior to the final vote on a text in plenary session. This action has been reduced in impact by the fact that the EP President can decide the explanations of vote will take place after the vote, when the room tends to be almost empty;
- Ask questions related to the work of Parliament's leadership functions;
- Table amendments to the Rules of Procedure;
- Raise points of order, which are limited to 1-minute interventions on any subject (since 2002);
- Move the inadmissibility of a matter;
- Make personal statements; and,
- Table an amendment at plenary, either as a Political Group or if signed by 40 MEPs (five percent of membership). Forty MEPs can also nominate candidates for the key roles in EP (President, Vice-President, Quaestor or Ombudsman); request roll call votes; oppose the adoption of reports without debate; and, through a so-called block vote,[20] table a motion for resolution at plenary level or propose to reject or amend a Council Common Position or the draft budget.

---

[20] In a block vote, MEPs must adopt or reject in one vote a whole series of amendments (and in some cases a Report in its entirety). This often happens if a report is either deemed non-controversial (to speed up voting) or a very tightly balanced compromise has been agreed on by the political groups. In the latter case, every amendment matters and a block vote avoids that the horse trading is disrupted by the adoption of one amendment requested by one political group, without its counterpart requested by another political group to reach the compromise.

- MEPs are first and foremost organised by political group. There are seven Europe-wide political groups, ranging from the strongly pro-federalist to the openly Eurosceptic, and from extreme left to extreme right.

- Within each political group, however, MEPs organise themselves by national delegation (especially the larger ones, such as France, UK, Germany), and in some cases the national solidarities can extend beyond party lines.

- Aside from its formal powers, the Parliament can also exercise a fair amount of pressure through the adoption of non-binding resolutions and Committee hearings, and general interaction with the press.

IF THEY OCCUPY SPECIFIC FUNCTIONS

(I) PRESIDENT OF THE EUROPEAN PARLIAMENT

(A) WHO?

The President is elected amongst candidates nominated either by Political Groups or upon a nomination signed by 40 MEPs. The election requires an absolute majority of MEP votes (unless there is still no result after three ballots, at which stage a simple majority is sufficient) and the President is usually elected for two and a half years.

(B) WHAT?

The EP President has quite a number of tasks (defined under Rule 19 of the Rules of Procedure), some of which can be delegated:

- Chair the European Parliament sittings, although in practice this is also done by the Vice-Presidents;
- Represent the EP in international relations, during ceremonial occasions and in administrative, legal or financial matters. There again, the extensive travel burden can be shared with the Vice-Presidents;
- Sign the budget into law;
- Co-sign with the President of the Council of the European Union all legislation adopted under co-decision procedure;

- Chair the Conference of Presidents (comprising the President of EP, Chairs of the political groups and two representatives of the non-attached MEPs, the latter not being allowed to vote) and Bureau meetings;
- Vote in the Bureau[21];
- Chair the Parliament's delegations in conciliation meetings with the Council in the framework of a third reading in the co-decision procedure, though this task is usually handled by the Vice-Presidents in charge of conciliation[22]; and,
- Right to attend and address the opening of the European Council meetings (which bring together the Heads of State or Government of the Member States at least four times per year).

The President is assisted by a cabinet of roughly twenty people (head, deputy head and administrators).

SURVIVAL TIP

The President plays an important role in the legislative process as he decides which Committees in the EP will handle a legislative measure proposed by the European Commission. The Commission does indicate which Committees it believes should handle it but it is the president that ultimately decides. For a lobbyist, this choice is important as every Committee in the EP has a different perspective on issues (the Industry Committee will for example look at things in a very different light than the Environment Committee).

(II) VICE-PRESIDENTS OF THE EUROPEAN PARLIAMENT

(A) WHO?

Fourteen Vice-Presidents are elected just after the President and their order of precedence, although of little practical importance, is determined by the number of votes they received.

---

[21] See page 47 for more details on the Bureau.
[22] See page 106 regarding the conciliation phase (or third reading) in co-decision.

(B) WHAT?

Their role consists of:

- Presiding over plenary sessions instead of the President;
- Representing the President at external functions; and,
- Taking part in the work of the Bureau.

Their tasks' division is based both on the weight of their Political Group and on special aptitudes.

(III) MEMBER OF THE CONFERENCE OF PRESIDENTS

(A) WHO?

In order to become part of the Conference of Presidents, an MEP has to be either the President of the EP, the Chair of a Political Group or one of the two non-attached MEPs allowed to participate in the Conference but without voting rights.

(B) WHAT?

Decisions are usually taken by consensus but occasionally weighted votes according to the number of members in each political party do occur as well.

The Conference meets at least twice a month behind closed doors, the meetings being prepared by the President's Cabinet, the Secretary-General of Parliament and the Secretaries-General of the Political Groups. Aside from its members, the Conference invites a representative of the Commission, of the Council and the chair of the Conference of Committee Chairs when discussing the draft agenda of the Parliament.

The Conference of Presidents sets the broad political direction of the European Parliament internally and externally but with practical implications.

This includes:

- The proposal as to which MEPs will be part of which Committees and Delegations, and the competence of the latter;
- The adjudication of disputes on competence between Committees;
- The authorisation to draft reports; and,
- The establishment of the draft agenda of the plenary sessions.

(IV) QUAESTORS

(A) WHO?

The six Quaestors are elected for two-and-a half-year terms after the President and fourteen Vice-Presidents. The functions are split between political parties according to their numeric weight, and taking into account the President's political affiliation.

They are also members of the Bureau and meet once a month.

(B) WHAT?

The Quaestors are responsible for the administrative and financial matters directly concerning MEPs and their working conditions.

This includes:

- Handling day-to-day issues related to the allocation of offices, exhibition authorisations, security, passes, and the allocation of services and equipment to MEPs (e.g. office equipment, allowances, vehicles, etc.); and,
- Present proposals to modify or rewrite rules presented by the Bureau as an advisory body.

SURVIVAL TIP

For a lobbyist, Quaestors are important in two respects: (1) they are the ones signing off EP access badges and it is thus always good to know at least one Quaestor and mention them as a reference on your badge application form and (2) they are respected by their colleague MEPs as they after all decide which PCs and other niceties MEPs receive as part of their EP package. This means an amendment tabled by them, for example, can always be useful.

(V) MEMBER OF THE BUREAU

(A) WHO?

The Bureau comprises the President of the EP, the fourteen Vice-Presidents and six Quaestors (but the latter only in an advisory capacity). The President holds the decisive vote in case of a tie. The Bureau usually meets twice a month.

(B) WHAT?

The Bureau has a vast scope of administrative and financial responsibilities that include:

- Appointing the Secretary-General;
- Handling all organisational issues related to the internal running of the EP, including staff policies, the organisation of sittings, and the authorisation of committee or delegation meetings outside the usual work places, as well as hearings, and fact-finding journeys by Rapporteurs; and,
- Make funding decisions for the EP's political parties and preparing the draft estimates of the EP's expenditure.

(VI) ROLES IN COMMITTEES: SUBSTITUTE, MEMBER, CHAIR, VICE-CHAIR OR COORDINATOR

(A) WHO?

Nearly every MEP is a member or substitute of one or more Committees. There are currently 20 standing committees, each focused on a specific sector and tasked with preparing dossiers relevant to that sector for plenary sittings. They are not all equal in terms of prestige or powers and their size (i.e. the number of members and substitutes composing them) is determined at the July session of the newly elected Parliament, and confirmed halfway through the European Parliament term.

Individual MEPs are assigned to Committees by their Political Groups (although they are also asked for their preferences).

Committees usually meet twice a month in Brussels for a few days or half days, during the weeks that follow plenary sittings in Strasbourg, although some short extra meetings are held in Strasbourg. Normal working hours are 3 pm to 6:30 pm and 9 am to 12:30 pm on the next day.

In addition to these standing Committees, the EP also has Temporary Committees, with a renewable 12-month mandate[23].

---

[23] For example, there has been a Climate Change Committee in the past and with the global crisis affecting the economy at present, there is a Financial, Economic and Social Crisis Committee.

Note that there is little difference in status between substitutes and full members: substitutes have full speaking rights and can vote in replacement of absent full members (which is not a rare occurrence).

Each Committee has one Chair and four Vice-chairs. The Chair has a considerable Committee influence as they can shape its agenda, speak at plenary sessions during sensitive votes, and represent the Committee at the Conference of Committee Chairs and at external functions. Their designation is done according to a very complex system referred to as the 'd'Hondt'[24]. It is a proportional representation system, with posts for chairs, vice-chairs, but also the leadership of the European Parliament being taken into account in a 'package deal', which leads to substantial horse trading.

Pick	EPP	Soc & Dem	ALDE	Greens / EFA	GUE/NGL	ECR	EFD
1	264	184	83	54	35	55	31
2	132	184	83	54	35	55	31
3	132	92	83	54	35	55	31
4	88	92	83	54	35	55	31
5	88	61.33	83	54	35	55	31
6	66	61.33	83	54	35	55	31
7	66	61.33	41.5	54	35	55	31
8	52.8	61.33	41.5	54	35	55	31
9	52.8	46	41.5	54	35	55	31
10	52.8	46	41.5	54	35	27.5	31
11	52.8	46	41.5	27	35	27.5	31
12	44	46	41.5	27	35	27.5	31
13	44	36.8	41.5	27	35	27.5	31
14	37.71	36.8	41.5	27	35	27.5	31
15	37.71	36.8	27.67	27	35	27.5	31
16	33	36.8	27.67	27	35	27.5	31
17	33	30.67	27.67	27	35	27.5	31
18	33	30.67	27.67	27	17.5	27.5	31
19	29.33	30.67	27.67	27	17.5	27.5	31
20	29.33	30.67	27.67	27	17.5	27.5	15.5
21	29.33	26.29	27.67	27	17.5	27.5	15.5
22	26.40	26.29	27.67	27	17.5	27.5	15.5

FIGURE 3 - SIMULATION OF D'HONDT SYSTEM APPLIED TO 2009-2014 EP - SOURCE: BURSON MARSTELLER[25]

---

[24] The 'd'Hondt method' is a highest averages method for allocating seats, named after the Belgian mathematician Victor D'Hondt. This system slightly favours large parties and coalitions over scattered small parties, as the bigger groups get first choices of committees over which their members will preside. The d'Hondt system is also applied inside the groups, the bigger national delegations (e.g. Germany) getting first choice within their political group.

[25] This simulation shows how the EPP gets the first choice of committee Chair, the Socialists & Democrats the second, the EPP the third as a result of its size compared to the next largest Group), and so on.

This system takes into account the weight of the Political Group for the chair allocation, and the weight of national delegations to designate the candidate, which all have a two-and-a-half-year term.

Less visible but certainly equally important are the Coordinators in each Committee. Each Political Group designates its Coordinator for individual Committees. They are the Group's main spokesperson for that Committee, and also in charge of negotiating how many points should be attributed to a Report and who will be put forward as Rapporteur if their group bids for it[26]. They assist Rapporteurs and Shadows in drafting voting recommendations and decide which substitutes can vote in the absence of full members. They also ensure that MEPs vote at critical times. Finding out who they are is not always evident. Some Political Groups list them on the Group's website, but in some cases it requires a bit of digging and asking around in the EP. Good sources of information are the Committee secretariat or the political advisors of the Political Groups.

(B) WHAT?

Committees prepare in their specialised area the work for plenary sessions.

This includes:

- Examining and proposing amendments to the Commission proposal of Directives and Regulations, either as lead committee (Report) or as secondary committees delivering an Opinion to the lead Committee. Note that the Commission's DG proposing draft legislation sends it to the committees, designating which one is responsible and which ones are consulted for an opinion. The DG's decision can be contested. Such contestation requires the intervention of the Conference of Presidents and, if no decision is reached within 6 working weeks, a vote at plenary; and,
- Producing draft own-initiative reports within a strict quota per committee, according to which each Committee can at any given time only have six parallel initiative reports under consideration.

---

[26] See page 50 regarding the role of Rapporteur.

Most of the work done by lobbyists in the EP happens at Committee level. The MEPs dealing with a measure in their Committee are likely to be more interested in a lobbyist's view on them than their colleagues not in that Committee and who will probably end up voting according to their political group's instructions in plenary.

(VII) ROLES IN A LEGISLATIVE PROCEDURE (RAPPORTEUR, DRAFTSMAN AND SHADOW RAPPORTEUR)

(A) WHO?

Rapporteurs are MEPs in charge of drawing up a report incorporating the amendments of the MEPs within the committee holding primary responsibility; Draftsmen hold the same role for the Opinions issued in secondary Committees.

The choice of Rapporteur depends on a complex system whereby each Political Group receives per Committee a quota of points according to its size. Each Report and Opinion then gets allocated a certain number of points by the Coordinators of each Committee, allowing the Political Groups to then bid for that Report or Opinion.

Theoretically, in case of multiple bids, the Political Group with the most points left in relation to the total number of points received (notional allocation), has priority. However, that rule is often discarded in practice and a lot of horse trading can occur on the side (e.g. an MEP entitled to a Report will give it to another MEPs, under the tacit agreement that the next Report in line is then given to the first MEP who happens to care more about that subject).

In terms of tactics, some Groups like to raise the stakes by bidding even when a Report is not really of interest to them. Or, in specialised areas, they might accept to give a Report to a specific MEP who is a recognised expert in the field at a cost of only a few points, just to make sure the best person deals with it (which is mostly the case in technical areas).

Regarding the annual budget and certain annual reports (e.g. the one on competition policy), each Group takes its turn in rotation.

Once a Rapporteur is designated, the other Political Groups generally designate their own Shadow Rapporteurs in charge of that Report for their Group and who have informal meetings with the Rapporteur to discuss amendments.

(B) WHAT?

The Rapporteur's role includes:

- Preparing initial discussions on a subject (often a legislative proposal); presenting a draft text with their suggested amendments; and providing voting recommendations (see a layout of a voting list in Annex 5) on the amendments presented by other MEPs;
- Presenting the report at plenary;
- Following developments after the first reading in case of co-decision procedure, preparing a recommendation for the second reading and participating in conciliation meetings[27]; and,
- Deciding on the timeline for a Report, especially when the other institutions ask for a speedy treatment or at the end of the Parliament's term.

Rapporteurs can be assisted by Committee staff, their own research assistants, their group's political advisors, staff within their constituency, research institutes and last but not least, lobbyists.

SURVIVAL TIP

Rapporteurs and Shadow Rapporteurs carry substantial weight in determining the course a legislative proposal will take. On many technical dossiers, they are nearly blindly followed by their colleague MEPs when it comes to voting on amendments (MEPs vote according to voting lists with '+' and '-' next to each numbered amendment, the Rapporteur's recommendation being present, and that of the Shadows being also distributed to their respective political group).

As a lobbyist, annoying the Rapporteur means that you face an uphill struggle in the EP for a dossier, something that should be avoided as much as possible. On the contrary, getting the Rapporteur on one's side can mean that many issues raised to their attention end up being presented as "Rapporteur" amendments, increasing the chance of success quite substantially.

In other words: make sure the Rapporteur and the Shadow Rapporteurs are your allies.

---

[27] See page 92 for the details of the co-decision procedure and its three readings.

(VIII) Roles in Delegations: Substitute, Member, Chair or Vice-Chair

(A) Who?

MEPs are also usually members of, or substitutes to at least one delegation, which ensure good working relationships with other parts of the world and especially the national Parliaments of countries outside the EU (e.g. USA, China, India, etc.).

Delegations meet once or twice a year, alternating between one of the EP's locations and at a venue decided by the national Parliament they are collaborating with. Preparatory meetings are held in Brussels or Strasbourg to set the agenda for these formal exchanges, and include the Ambassadors of the concerned countries and members of the European Commission.

Each delegation has a Chair and usually two Vice-Chairs, nominated for two-and-a-half-year terms. As is the case with Committees, their nomination is based on the d'Hondt system[28]. This sometimes results in certain Political Groups holding chairmanship of a delegation to the great dismay of the other country concerned, resulting in some extreme cases in a refusal to collaborate with a given delegation for several years. This is especially true for delegations that handle relations with countries such as Israel or Palestine, where sensitivities are high.

Knowing that an MEP is on a specific delegation can be of interest if it's the country of origin of the stakeholder you represent. You could for example suggest a visit to the headquarters or a dinner with the MEP when they visit the country in question.

(B) What?

Delegations maintain relations and exchange information with parliaments in non-EU countries, notably:

- They ensure that the EP is represented abroad, as a counterweight to the role of the Commission and the Council;
- They exchange information with other parliaments, to spread their own message but also to learn from other practices;
- They monitor elections and assess the respect of human rights;

---

[28] See page 47.

- They allow Parliament to discuss EU accession with candidate countries; and,
- Their Chair submits summary reports (always in writing for inter-parliamentary delegations, sometimes orally for the other types of delegations) about delegation meetings to the Foreign Affairs Committee, and where appropriate, to the Development Committee.

Delegations must coordinate in general with the Committees in Parliament on relevant subjects.

A subset of delegations includes the so-called 'Parliamentary Assemblies', namely: ACP-EU, Euro-Mediterranean, Euronest and the Euro-Latin American one.

4.   WHY WOULD THEY CARE ABOUT YOUR ISSUE?

Approaching an MEP has to be carefully evaluated. They might care about your client's for multiple reasons:

- Because of their nationality and, even more specifically, the constituency they represent within the Parliament. If, for instance, your client represents an industry, which crucially supplies many jobs to the voters of an MEP's home constituency, the politician in question will most likely be easier to approach and willing to listen;
- Because of their membership to specific Committees or delegations;
- Because of their past careers. Some MEPs were teachers, whilst others have worked in various companies and therefore developed an in-depth understanding of the industries they were employed in (which does not always imply an affinity); and,
- Because of a 'pet' interest, revealed in past press releases, interventions, motions, questions, etc.

The turnover in MEPs from one election to another (and even between elections) is high and averages just under 50 percent. Moreover, less than five percent of MEPs have EP careers stretching 15 years or beyond.

In practice, this means the contacts made in the European Parliament must be renewed on a regular basis. But it also means in some cases that the MEP you knew in Brussels can become a valuable contact for their home country – hence the importance of maintaining good relationships. Once their EP term is over, many MEPs pursue very active political careers as Ministers, Prime Ministers and even Presidents or take on European affairs roles. Some actually pendle back and forth between the EP and a national role.

C. MEP ASSISTANTS

1. WHO ARE THEY?

MEPs receive a secretarial allowance to employ staff and pretty much use it as it pleases them. This means that whilst some MEPs prefer to hire two well-paid policy assistants, others pick more secretarial/office management types, or use a combination of both. The assistants can be based in Brussels, the MEP's constituency or the MEP's national capital.

Assistants are usually young (often freshly graduated from University) and most of them stay only for a short period.

Only a small number of the assistants stay in the Parliament for several years, either for the same MEP or switching from one MEP to another.

2. WHERE ARE THEY?

Even if some assistants are adepts of the plenary sessions in Strasbourg, many others do not necessarily accompany their MEP to every single meeting. In fact, there is somewhat of a split between MEP assistants keen to follow their MEP around and those who stay at the office in Brussels or in the home country.

This means that plenary weeks in Strasbourg can be a good time to find assistants more relaxed in Brussels and willing to have a chat or coffee, with their boss being stuck in endless plenary votes 450 km away.

3. WHAT DO THEY DO?

Assistants' tasks vary greatly and may include:

- Preparing the policy and political dossiers for an MEP, notably by conducting background research;
- Handling logistics ranging from administrative work to booking tickets, running errands, securing visitor badges, and arranging meetings with Commission officials or lobbyists;
- Handling relationships with the MEPs constituents;
- Handling correspondence: reading the hundreds of emails most MEPs receive per day and draft responses or letters;
- Drafting articles, press releases, amendments, parliamentary questions; and,
- Representing MEPs in first meetings with lobbyists or other stakeholders, as a sort of 'filter' or gatekeeper.

They can thus be key elements in the decision-making process and should never be disregarded, no matter how seemingly minor their role might be. After all, regardless of their function, a vast majority of them read the emails their MEPs receive and you would not want them to hit "delete" too soon.

4. WHY WOULD THEY CARE ABOUT YOUR ISSUE?

MEP assistants know that their bosses have hectic schedules and do not like to see their time wasted.

They will care about you if:

- Your arguments are concise, well-structured, easy-to-use (e.g. in a language that allows them to claim authorship to their boss or copy-paste bits in their own memos and summaries), properly formatted and allow them to shine and/or make their boss look good;
- You have something to offer in exchange: third parties outside the EP often gain access to documents from other institutions faster than actual staff of the institutions. Sharing that info with assistants, pointing them in the right direction, showing willingness to respond to questions that might not be related to a dossier you are involved in, etc., which makes them care; and,
- You make them feel as important as their boss.

- About fifteen former assistants ended up becoming MEPs themselves.

- Some assistants combine a part-time function of assistant with the running of their own consultancy. This is perfectly allowed as long as they declare in writing to the Parliament secretariat all of the additional remunerations obtained from their activities outside the Parliament. This Special Register of Financial Interests is publicly available and worth checking from time to time, to prevent wasting your time on an assistant that happens to do consulting work for a stakeholder with opposite interests.

D. POLITICAL GROUPS

1. WHO ARE THEY?

EP Members are organised first and foremost according to their political affiliation.

To that end, the Parliament is split in seven different Political Groups, going from extreme left to extreme right, and from the pro-federalists to the Eurosceptics (not to mention the Europhobes).

Several rules have to be taken into account in order to create a Political Group:

- The Group must include at least 25 Members from at least one-quarter of the EU's countries, which means seven Member States (Rule 30 of the Rules of Procedure).

- The Group does not necessarily have to be made up of one single political party, but the participating parties must share some 'political affinity'.

Once recognised, political groups have the right to receive subsidies from the parliament, as well as guaranteed seats on Committees, including a quota of leading positions.

The current EP Political Groups are:

- European People's Party (EPP);

- Progressive Alliance of Socialists and Democrats (S&D);

- Alliance of Liberals and Democrats for Europe (ALDE);

- Greens-European Free Alliance (Greens / EFA);

- European Conservatives and Reformists (ECR);

- European United Left / Nordic Green Left (UEN / NGL); and,

- Europe of Freedom and Democracy (EFD).

SURVIVAL TIP

The EP also has so-called 'Intergroups', which are informal groups of MEPs from different political groups. These intergroups are not organs of the EP but can, if officially recognised, benefit from EP meeting and translation facilities.

There are 20 official cross-party intergroups united on issues such as animal welfare, disabilities and anti-racism, and about 20 non-registered ones such as the Kangaroo group that promotes freedom of movement. Given their size, some intergroups are either assisted by the secretariat of a political group or have their own administration.

Lobbyists can get involved in the running of such intergroups, which are very interesting places to shape the vision and take part in the discussion on certain issues.

---

2. WHERE ARE THEY?

Political Groups sit with the Parliament, even though some of their meetings are held outside of the Brussels/Strasbourg axis (with some criticism from third parties when the location is very exotic).

3. WHAT DO THEY DO?

The political groups hold regular meetings during the week before the plenary session and during plenary week, as well as seminars to determine the main principles of their EU activity. They have a staff of political advisors which, as outlined in the following pages, play an important role.

- Several political groupings have founded political parties that operate at European level, e.g. the European People's Party, the Party of European Socialists, the European Green Party and the European Liberal Democrat and Reform Party. They work in close cooperation with the corresponding political groups within Parliament.
- The non-attached (or "NI" for the French "non-inscrits") MEPs are all those that are not members of any recognised political group. The non-attached rarely intervene at Committee level but have been known to try to make an impact at plenary sessions.
- The permanent staff of political groups, and notably the political advisors, can play a key role in shaping policies, especially on less politically visible issues.

E.   POLITICAL ADVISORS AND OTHER POLITICAL STAFF

1.   WHO ARE THEY?

Political Groups are entitled to specifically allocated staff, in relation to their size and the number of working languages used within the Group.

This has meant that large Groups such as the EPP have been attributed over 270 staff members, whereas smaller groups can have only 30. In practice, this also means that larger political groups can have several advisors following the same Committee while smaller groups might have one advisor following the work of several Committees, making the task quite difficult.

The vast majority of Political Group employees are temporary agents, which means they do not enjoy the same job security as the permanent officials. On the upside, they are designated by the political parties without having to go through the open competitions system.

2.   Where are they?

Political advisors have offices in Brussels and Strasbourg but do not follow their Group to Strasbourg if, for example, the plenary session will not feature matters of interest to them.

3.   What do they do?

Political advisors have usually both general and sector-specific responsibilities and, through their tasks, play an important role in shaping the decisions made by a political group:

- They follow what happens within the Committees;
- They prepare discussions and supply background information for their group meetings;
- They assist in the formulation of a Group position before plenary sessions;
- They physically gather MEPs from other Committees to vote as substitutes when a Committee vote is too tight to call;
- They keep in touch with national parties, Commissioners of their political colour and other organisations; and,
- They meet with lobbyists.

SURVIVAL TIP

Political advisors to Committees are certainly worth meeting when a legislative measure you are interested in is handled by that Committee.

In many cases, even if the Rapporteur is involved hands-on in a Report, they leave the assessment of less important issues to the appreciation of the political advisor who decides how important the matter issue is and, more importantly, whether it should receive a positive or negative voting recommendation on the voting list.

Political advisors tend to invest a lot of time into individual dossiers and should therefore be approached with sound and well-formed arguments. They are not afraid of delving into technical matters and should certainly not be underestimated.

F.   SECRETARIAT AND OTHER EP STAFF

1.   WHO ARE THEY?

The EP has about 6,000 employees, a third of which sit in the linguistic services. Political advisors to the Political Groups are also employees of the Parliament.

DIRECTORATE-GENERALS

DG Presidency	Responsible for the organisation of plenary, relations with national parliaments, the Conference of Presidents, the Bureau, the Quaestors. Includes the Tabling Office that judges the admissibility of amendments.
DG Internal Policies	Provides the support staff for Committees
DG External Policies	Assists the Committee responsible for external policies and the delegations and acts as a link between the interparliamentary delegations, non-EU countries and parliaments throughout the world
DG Communication	Handles media relations and provides MEPs with a library and documentation service

Legal Service

EP PRESIDENT — **Secretary General**

Secretary-General's Office

DG Personnel
DG Infrastructure and Logistics
DG Translation
DG Interpretation & Conferences
DG Finances
DG Innovation & Technological Support

FIGURE 4 - MAIN DIRECTORATES-GENERAL OF THE EP SECRETARIAT

The Political Groups have little or no influence on most of the EP staff appointments, except for the higher levels (Director and Director-General) that are appointed by the Bureau of the Parliament, composed of MEPs of all Political Groups[29].

The civil servants working in the general-secretariat are supposed to carry out their duties in a politically neutral way. Oddly enough, they are nevertheless allowed to be members of Political Groups or even to stand for election, the only prerequisite for the latter being that they take temporary leave.

Moreover, it is not unusual for staff from Political Groups to move on to the general-secretariat, and vice versa.

---

[29] See page 47 for more details regarding the Bureau.

2.   WHERE ARE THEY?

Members of the secretariat are true jet setters, with individual offices in either Luxembourg (official seat of the secretariat) or Brussels, as well as shared offices in Strasbourg.

3.   WHAT DO THEY DO?

The staff includes interpreters, secretaries, administrators, translators, assistants, clerical staff and manual or service staff.

At the head is the EP's highest official, the Secretary-General, who gets appointed by the Bureau.

Under their supervision, the tasks are split into eight DGs and a Legal Service, all headed by a Director-General and subdivided into Directorates.

Each European Parliament Committee has its own permanent staff or 'secretariat' made up of four to ten administrators and one Head of Unit.

A Committee's secretariat can play a considerable role in shaping the work of that Committee. It is not unusual to see a Rapporteur rely more heavily on Committee staff than on his own assistants, simply because of the experience the employees have in the areas the Committee specialises in.

Their tasks notably cover:

- Briefing MEPs on past positions of the Committee;
- Conducting background research on a given Report; and,
- Helping in the drafting of Reports.

Their assignment to certain tasks or dossiers depends on their expertise, as well as their linguistic skills in relation to the languages spoken by a given Rapporteur.

4.   WHY WOULD THEY CARE ABOUT YOUR ISSUE?

As Parliament officials are supposed to look at issues from a politically-neutral perspective, the main arguments to convince them are usually technical by nature, especially as regards the Committee secretariats.

You are most likely to win their support if you present them with a well-informed briefing which takes into consideration the fact that they cover a broad range of topics and discussions on a day-to-day basis.

FACTS & STATS

A recently introduced 'mobility' policy entails that all parliament staff is supposed to change roles on a regular basis, normally every three years for junior employees and seven years for more senior posts. In other words, once they finally got to grips with the issues they need to address, they are moved to another position. At the same time, however, this new policy has put an end to the scenario of one official staying in the job for decades - which was great if the official liked you and hell if you were not on their Christmas cards list.

CHAP. 2: HOW?
MULTIPLE DIMENSIONS, LOBBYIST TYPOLOGY & THE RULES OF THE GAME

I. INTRODUCTION

What's the secret to successful lobbying? Sadly, there is no magical formula.

The 'how' is probably the most complex question to answer because it involves taking into account so many different aspects that it will send an average human over the brink of sanity...unless they are a professional lobbyist, in which case they will actually enjoy dealing with multi-layered approaches.

Lobbyists (and their lobby targets) thrive on playing complex chess parties likely to puzzle the grand master Kasparov himself[30].

It is important to realise that there are two sides to the lobbying ecosystem: the targets of lobbying and the lobbyist. The "who" Chapter addresses the former. As regards the latter, it is useful to understand the different types of lobbyists and lobby techniques available.

This section outlines some of the intricacies of the lobbying art, namely:

- The multiple dimensions of EU lobbying in terms of national, political, institutional and human aspects;
- The different types of lobbyists hurrying across the cobblestone pavements of the Place du Luxembourg (where the EP is located) and haunt the EU institutions' corridors; and,
- Some of the do's and don'ts to keep in mind when lobbying in Brussels.

---

[30] As I stated in the Foreword to this book, I believe curling makes a better comparison.

THE 3Ps: PEOPLE, POWER & PROCEDURES

To be perfectly accurate, lobbying in Brussels actually requires a rule of 5Ps: people, power, and procedures, but also patience and persistence, which are crucial to achieving success on the EU scene.

One learns quite quickly in Brussels that you do not lobby institutions: you lobby people. Obviously, the way in which you lobby them might be influenced by the institution they represent, but at the end of the day, in many cases, their willingness to support or ignore you is intrinsically linked to whether they trust and like you. The people rule is simple but cruel: it takes months to build a reputation and seconds to destroy it.

The balance of power is a second crucial element and refers to both the obvious power games between institutions, and the power equilibrium within an institution. Does a dossier overlap different European Commission Directorates-General or EP Committees? Do the Commissioners responsible for this issue like each other or not? Who would you prefer to see lead? Are you more likely to succeed if the lead lies in one place rather than another? None of these questions are easy to answer but knowing the right answer can have a crucial impact on your strategy.

Procedures in turn sound like a major turn off. After all, who cares about procedures? Well, probably no one, but they are quite frankly one of the deadliest tools that can be used against you. Especially in the EP, procedures are used, abused and sometimes seem to have been purely invented to serve the needs of the most powerful MEPs in a legislative process. As an assistant once told me, "If you know the people at the Tabling Office and in the secretariats, you can make or break an amendment in a snap." Procedural excuses are often used to try to discourage lobbyists from pushing an issue. It is therefore essential to familiarise yourself with the EP's 216 Rules of Procedure and its multiple Annexes. Being able to understand and interpret them will help you fight procedure with procedure.

Finally, the combination of patience and persistence is the most difficult to attain, but also the most rewarding: nothing in Brussels goes as quickly as you'd want to. This can be very frustrating for the business people you deal with as a lobbyist, as the pace of things tends to be depressingly slow.

But, at the same time, the virtue of patience needs to be combined with a serious dose of persistence. One of the most common sentences you're likely to hear in Brussels is "That is impossible", closely followed by "We will see what we can do" (with the silent "euh...nothing" implied) Persistence is something most Europeans are not good at, and that I personally learnt from my American clients – who in turn are terrible at playing the patience game skilfully mastered by Europeans (probably as a result of our more inefficient environment). Know your 5Ps and Brussels could be yours!

II.   The Multiple dimensions of EU lobbying

There are multiple ways to look at, and approach the EU. In fact, the European policy-making scene has political, national and institutional dimensions.

As a lobbyist in Brussels, you need to carefully analyse these three key dimensions and try to understand how each of them can be used to obtain the targeted result.

A.   Political dimension

The most obvious symptom of the political dimension is the fact that the EP is organised around Political Groups. In some cases, the affiliation of national parties to these European political groups can be surprising. For example, the Belgian 'Centre démocrate humaniste'[31] party which would be ranked as a rather leftist party in Belgium, is part of the Conservative EPP Political Group in the European Parliament, which leans to the right of the political spectrum.

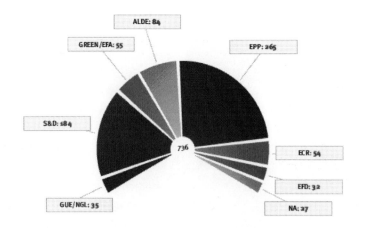

Figure 5-Seat Repartition per political group in the EP after 2009 elections (2009-2014 legislature)

---

[31] The Humanist Democratic Centre (Centre démocrate humaniste or cdH) is a Belgian Francophone Christian democratic political party in the French-speaking part of Belgium.

For some issues, the weight of a European Political Group acting in unison can be tremendous. On other issues, voting can occur according to a purely national logic, across Political Groups.

Political affiliations also extend beyond the EP: Commissioners belong to certain political families, as do the governments of Member states. All these affiliations play a role. In some cases, it means that the MEPs of a certain country will vote in a different direction than their government because they are from a different political side. Sometimes, certain permanent representations of the Member States only brief MEPs who share the same political affiliation as their government, leaving the others blatantly in the dark or, even worse, misinforming them. Finally, Commissioners stemming from the bigger European Political Groups will gain a larger support in the EP than others, especially on more controversial measures.

B. NATIONAL DIMENSION

National interests will nearly always prevail over Political Group interests, when it comes to voting behaviour in the EP.

But even in the European Commission, Commissioners never forget the country they come from (and are likely to go back to, once their term as Commissioner ends).

This national dimension is crucial when approaching decision-makers: why would a Commissioner help you if you have nothing to offer to their country or, even worse, if your goal could prove detrimental to the interests of one of your competitors based in the Commissioner's home country? Things are not always as clear-cut, but they do often tend to boil down to these basics. In some cases, moral grounds will make the difference. There are some exceptions though, especially in global sectors such as the Internet, where politicians can be persuaded to take an interest simply because they make use of a service. As an MEP once told me: "I use this application to video-chat with my grand-children every week; of course, I'm interested in hearing about the issues that could affect it!"

The national dimension is also important in the way one interacts with decision-makers. Lobbying is not perceived in the same manner from one country to another, and ignoring this can lead to some serious clashes.

A 2009 report on *Effective Lobbying in Europe* by the international lobbying firm Burson-Marsteller revealed that Spanish, French and German MEPs for example appreciate being approached by a lobbyist from their respective country, or at least defending an issue of national interest (see Figure 6). Meanwhile, Scandinavian MEPs will find this less crucial.

How important is it that you are approached by someone of your own nationality on an issue of national interest?

	All	AT	CZ	DE	DK	FI	FR	GR	HU	IT	NL	NO	PL	SE	ES	UK	EU
Very important	16	21	4	19	6	27	30	27	6	13	4	3	4	28	39	16	6
Quite important	34	38	53	39	32	43	53	53	27	30	33	23	23	10	58	16	27
Not very important	28	25	20	23	39	27	17	17	30	20	40	42	43	23	3	34	38
Not at all important	22	16	23	19	23	3	0	3	37	37	23	32	30	39	0	34	29

FIGURE 6 – HOW IMPORTANT IS IT FOR MEPs TO BE APPROACHED BY SOMEONE OF THEIR OWN NATIONALITY – SOURCE: BURSON-MARSTELLER REPORT ON 'EFFECTIVE LOBBYING IN EUROPE', P. 28

Finally, from the Council's point of view, the national factor is crucial because votes are weighted differently from one country to another. Though most decisions are taken by consensus, this does affect discussions as certain Member States use their weight to pressure smaller countries into following their lead.

This implies that the time and effort you put into lobbying Member states is calibrated against the number of votes a country holds, except when your strategy is to obtain a blocking minority whereby a cluster of smaller Member States 'hold the Council hostage'[32].

C.   INSTITUTIONAL DIMENSION

As previously mentioned, Europe is built on an institutional triangle. This dimension intrinsically influences every dossier, every position and every new initiative taken at European level. Missing the institutional dimension in a lobbying strategy is a sure way to fail in your enterprise. A great example of this is the way in which both the Council and the United States of America handled the (in)famous SWIFT dossier in February 2010.

In short, this dossier concerned an agreement reached between the EU governments in Council and the US, whereby the latter were allowed to access bank data of European citizens. The institutional dimension was ill-assessed

---

[32] See page 24 for a detailed overview of the Council voting mechanism.

because it failed to take into consideration that, under the new Lisbon Treaty, the EP had to approve this agreement. The agreement as initially put forward by the European Commission and Council ended up being rejected by the EP. On a side note, a last minute-lobbying push from US Vice-President Joe Biden and Secretary of State Hillary Clinton indicated that the parties involved had finally (though too late) recognised that the EP could no longer be disregarded in such matters.

For an industry lobbyist, the institutional dimension implies a good understanding of who can do what (not only in terms of rules, but also in terms of practice, moral power, horse trading capabilities, etc.) and a constant exchange with all three institutions, to ensure that all are kept informed.

III. The different types of lobbyists on the Brussels Mole Hill

This section will focus on how lobbyists can be used for different purposes, regardless of whether they are in-house employees or hired on a consultancy basis.

A. The Jack of all Trades

Many public affairs companies cater to all needs and across industries. Agriculture, chemicals, telecoms, fisheries...you name it, they cover it.

Unfortunately, this Jack-of-all-trades approach often translates into the master-of-none follow-up, unless the firm is big enough to feature specialised departments for every area. It also often creates some very specific lobbying behaviour, discussed in the sections below.

1. The Parrot

Many companies still think that lobbyists are just very articulate used car sales people who repeat their pitch ad nauseam to anyone who wants to listen (or is unlucky enough to get cornered in a hallway). And doubtlessly, there are indeed a fair number of lobbyists who rely primarily on their gift of the gab and forego substance for form.

The parrot lobbyist switches seamlessly between advocating energy-saving light bulbs, supporting the use of pesticides in agriculture, and pushing for the fact that spectrum freed up from the digital dividend should be given to broadcasters. They usually know very little about the actual analysis, background research and/ or technical details of the issue at stake.

But does that mean the parrot lobbyist is inefficient? Well not necessarily, as long as you use them in the right places (e.g. do not bring them to a technical DG meeting) and with the right people (e.g. an MEP after 7 pm, requiring only an elevator pitch or a cocktail napkin drawing). Moreover, the parrot lobbyist shares with its namesake mascot not only the ability to replicate text and intonation, but also a certain feather flamboyance (usually expressed by Armani suits).

A major limitation with the parrot lobbyist, however, is that you can usually only let them meet the same person **once**. Chances are they would run out of debate ammunition during a second encounter. You also need to make sure your parrot is smart enough to admit ignorance when quizzed on a certain subject they lack knowledge about.

2. THE DOOR OPENER

The Door opener is usually a grey-haired ex-something (Commissioner, MEP, MP, take your pick) and knows a lot of people or claims he or she does (the proof is in the pudding). As a result, they are hired for **who** they know, not **what** they know. They can be of great value, by opening the door to people and offices that would otherwise remain unattainable to your lobbying efforts. They are particularly useful for smaller to medium companies, which tend to be too unknown or small to gain access to the ivory towers of Commissioners or Ministers. The Door Opener, who is a former colleague/ university pal or current personal friend of Mr X, makes one phone call and you've got yourself an appointment the next morning.

Still, caution is advised with Door Openers who occasionally do not keep their promise of delivering results or do it in a way not necessarily helpful to the client. For instance, you do not have direct access to Commissioner or Minister X, but Mr or Mrs Door Opener guarantees they have raised your issue with said Minister at their monthly one-on-one dinner. What they fail to mention is that they have also raised a zillion other issues relating to a zillion other clients at that same dinner, meaning yours probably got lost somewhere between dessert and coffee.

In essence, the Door Opener is most useful if they actually introduce you to Minister X in person and let you do your own pitch – unless you trust them to have your best interests at heart, or your case is genuinely best served if the Door Opener has a private meeting with Minister X to ask them for a favour. Otherwise, you should question their commitment to aid your interest if they refuse to create a direct link between you and Minister X. Finally, paying someone to open the door and then not ensuring that it is kept open truly is a waste of time and money, unless you are handling a major crisis and just need a guerrilla operation in a Minister's office! Lobbying is about building relationships and hence keeping doors open (if not ajar at least) for the long term.

B. THE ASSOCIATION / COALITION ANIMATOR

Some lobbying firms seem to specialise in the management of associations and coalitions (or 'lobbying vehicles'), which are an important element in the Brussels landscape. In general, these 'association' managers try to stick to a certain theme (i.e. food or Internet), which reflects their own personal expertise and/or network. But some of them seem to think that running an association is much more about handling mailing lists and doing the odd update on an uninspiring website, than understanding the issues at stake and leveraging an existing network of contacts to the benefit of the association.

Running an association is often a very painful experience, especially if you happen to be a lobbyist with a certain sense of pride and the willingness to achieve something. This is basically due to the way associations are built and grown in Brussels (and probably everywhere where lobbying is a job and not just a hobby). Due to the need to claim that your association is representative, and in order to be able to afford a part- or full-time lobbyist representing the association, associations often bring together companies that are not necessarily like-minded on many topics. For the lobbyist in charge of the association, this means threading on difficult territory when responding to consultation or writing statements on behalf of the association, as every member has to the agree on every word in these documents. This has an impact in terms of timing (draft position papers must be circulated to all members at an early stage for everyone to have sufficient time to react, with often second, third and more revised drafts until a compromise is reached) and content of the statements (as stakeholders with different interests tend to neutralise each other, associations that are too large often end up with very bland non-committal position papers).

Associations can be classified as follows:

- The Fake: it has a website, articles, a secretariat, a series of members belonging to one big multi-national (often American) with a set of SMEs and academics, and no indication of membership fee or funding transparency page. This is clearly an association set up by one single company looking to either get enhanced credibility through an associative vehicle or not linking its own name directly to an issue by using an umbrella;

- The Lame but Rich: this type of association has a high representativity factor, as it includes more than a hundred members of a given sector or with a shared interest. But, as explained above, given their sheer number, the many companies also often have competing or diverging interests. As a result, the association is bound to primarily produce dull and neutralised position papers. On the upside, it does however put together great cocktail events and issues a glossy annual report that makes for boring and predictable reading. The secretariat is overstaffed and the head of the association usually spends their life going from one conference to another, preferably in exotic locations. Members' main reason for joining is to ensure that the association does not get captured by one company's specific set of interests. In addition the membership fees allow for some fine wining and dining; and,

- The Focused but Fragile: unlike the previous one, this association brings together a small number of companies that agree on a joint stance about a small selection of issues. It is often an ad hoc coalition whose members try to pool together resources without necessarily hiring a secretariat or spokesperson. The advantage is that it is a low-cost formula, which usually produces some strong positions. The less positive side to it is that usually, only a handful of companies do the work and act as association representatives. This can sometimes lead to an over-emphasis of certain interests specific to these businesses, hence removing the 'umbrella' factor.

C. THE SPECIALIST OR BOUTIQUE LOBBYIST

For the sake of transparency, I need to reveal that I myself am a so-called boutique lobbyist. In practice, this is someone who focuses on a given sector and has normally worked in that sector (either as an industry employee or as a policy maker/regulator or both). They can therefore easily assess the potential impact of a given issue and develop a sound 'sales pitch' aimed at both technical experts and politicians involved in the decision-making process.

Usually, each sector counts about a dozen of such freelance specialists, many of whom work in-house for a major company. Their main challenge is handling conflict of interests and juggling multiple hats. They usually bring credibility to the dossiers they handle, and their network is likely to cover exactly those people who need to be approached on a given issue. Finding a boutique lobbyist usually happens solely on a word-of-mouth basis, as most serious boutique lobbyists do not spend much time on business development or advertising. Instead, they get things done. Companies come to them either because they know them directly or because they were referred by either colleagues from other firms, sector-specific associations or even policy-makers (who usually know who they like to be lobbied by).

THE GOLDEN RULES WHEN HIRING A LOBBYIST

1. If you are hiring a multi-consultant firm, ask who precisely will work on your account. Beware of brilliant pitch teams that make a great impression but actually end up never working on your account, leaving it to the less inspiring colleagues. Similarly, when they present you the team that will work on your account, talk to the most junior member in the room: they're likely to be the ones doing the most work anyway.

2. If they say they can do everything and more, they are usually lying or have a breadth of staff expertise that is exceptional. Be reassured by a lobbyist that admits they cannot deliver certain elements of a strategy but can put you in contact with people who could.

3. If a lobbyist says he does not need to know the details of your issue or that he does not truly need to believe it, get up slowly and run away like never before.

4. If you wouldn't buy it, they won't either. Don't just brief your lobbyist: ask them to brief you on how they will sell your case. If they do not sound convincing, there is no way they will convince policy-makers either.

5. If you are member of a trade association, ask that association which lobbyist they would recommend. Associations usually know most specialised lobbyists and have a good overview of their skills (except if the trade association is run by a lobbying firm, in which case the answer may not be very objective.

6. If a lobbyist's idea of preparing an outreach programme for you is a road show to meet as many of his MEP and Commission 'friends' they can put before you, instead of ensuring you meet the right targets, beware. Brussels is not a numbers game but one of careful marksmanship.

7. Do not accept mystery tales from lobbyists, unless they present you with a leaked document or information for which you would expect them to protect their source. For all other matters, ask for names and contact details and have open discussions about who you can contact directly and who is better left as a direct contact of your lobbyist (because they have a relationship with them or special affinities such as nationality).

8. Try to avoid hiring lobbyists for 'fly in and fly out' operations that put them in a 'fire fighting' only scenario. Being on the ground on a continuous basis is often cheaper than ad hoc damage control operations, and bears more fruits.

IV. Rules of the Jungle: the Do's and Don'ts of the EU Lobbyists

Contrary to common belief, the Brussels Jungle is governed by laws which go well beyond the mere 'survival-of-the-fittest' principle. These rules range from professional efficiency to elementary politeness, and should not be ignored if you are hunting for success.

A. Lobby at every level: Bottom-up, Top Down and anything in the middle

Would you try to climb a tree from the top? Many lobbyists strategies seem to assume that convincing the people at the top is enough, never mind the foot soldiers!

The problem is that, in most cases, the top people are politicians, and that politicians, well, do politics. In other words, they see dossiers in a manner that is totally different to lobbyists and it is not unusual for trade-offs to happen at political level between two issues that are totally unrelated and hence unforeseeable for a lobbyist. Disappointed once by the representative of a ministry withdrawing his support to an amendment I had fought for, I was told by that representative that the government had made a trade-off between that amendment in the telecoms sector and another one they felt more strongly about in an agriculture-related dossier. This means politicians are highly unpredictable and rarely end up delivering results at the level of detail or in the exact format required by businesses. Unfortunately, you will often need their helping hand (or even just their friendly indifference) to get civil servants to budge for instance.

It's important to bear in mind that the 'foot soldiers' at the bottom of a hierarchy are nevertheless often those who control access to the highest levels. Ignoring them (or bypassing them entirely) can often result in them hitting the delete button when your email pops up in their boss' mailbox.

Everyone in the legislative food chain has a specific function, from the assistant juggling with the constraints of their boss' schedule, to the Commissioner in charge of a portfolio affecting nearly 500 million Europeans- they all have a role to play. Understand it, respect it but more importantly, respect each of them.

Does that mean you should ignore the top and go for the lower branches? Not at all. It just means that every branch is important and that it's worth paying attention to everyone involved in the decision-making process.

Make also sure to feed them arguments that mean something in their world. Statistics, charts and other mind-numbing tools work well with the economist in charge of the impact assessment of a legislation at draft stage, whereas an MEP will in most cases be more concerned about jobs (especially amongst their electoral constituency) and growth for the European economy.

Also, do not fall for the assumption (often created by the European Commission itself) that the European Commission just proposes legislation and that you should then lobby Parliament and Council. Each of the three institutions matters at every step, especially within a co-decision procedure.

The best strategies are those where a company is smart enough to access the highest levels through "door opener" lobbyists while specialist lobbyists assisted by the relevant business and/or technical people, set out their arguments at the working level. This ensures that the right 'good will' is present at the top and that the levels under it consider that the dossier can pass on its merit too. I must also point out that, in my experience, few companies are willing to put the means in place to implement a 'loving-squeeze' strategy, whereby upper and lower management meet in the middle, with all the levels properly covered and briefed.

B.   THE USE OF COMMON SENSE

Common sense and manners, manners, manners at all times.

Remember how your mum told you to say please to the lady and thank you to the gentleman? Well, the same rules of conduct apply inside the metal and glass constructions of the European institutions hosting numerous decision-makers. Politeness is quintessential in the lobbying business.

So a few obvious tips:

- Don't try to stop an MEP obviously in a hurry because the voting bell for plenary just rang;
- Don't follow someone into the toilet (I actually saw that happen and it's kind of scary, frankly);
- Don't 'poke', or throw a sheep at them on Facebook;
- Don't think that they owe you anything: there is nothing in the Rules of Procedure of Parliament that oblige an MEP to respond positively to a meeting request, nor do the internal rules of the Commission or the Better Regulation principles say anything about the need to physically meet each and every lobbyist that knocks at their door;

- Make an appointment instead of barging into someone's office; send them your position beforehand so that they can be properly prepared or briefed if they wish to; check out if there is anything specific they want to talk about; and, even if you just had the worst meeting of your life, thank them for taking the time to see you and try to part in a friendly manner, because you never know if you might not need them in the future;
- Meet them when you don't need them (yet), but try not to waste their time either; and,
- And if you are going to nag them about an issue, at least keep your sense of humour and make them smile. The EU bubble gets easily afraid when faced with too much intensity and passion, and seems to prefer a more laidback and slightly cynical approach.

C.   STRATEGIES

In terms of picking a single or multiple strategies, it can be useful to take a walk on the wild side. In the jungle, every animal has a certain behavioural reputation which, as a lobbyist in the Brussels jungle, has led me to identify the following strategies to conduct a lobbying effort:

- The Boa: don't bite but smother them to the point of status quo...and death. Basically do not oppose legislation but delay it, weaken it and squeeze out any air it had in it, with no true hostilities but a nice strangling motion. For example, advocate for the need to establish a Task Force with a Steering Committee that aims at achieving international standardisation and the voluntary adoption of a Code of Conduct by industry... All these intermediary steps sound very constructive but result in pushing a dossier down the slow lane (and in some case end up killing it completely). Sounds familiar?

- The Duck-Flight: The reason ducks fly together in a V-like formation is twofold. First, because the shape of the formation reduces the drag force that each bird experiences when it flies alone. Secondly, it allows the birds to communicate more easily and keep the flock together. It's pretty much the same thing in lobbying: using trade associations or ad hoc coalitions can often be more effective to get your point across as it creates broader representation for your issue and allows spreading the message through multiple sources.

- The Camouflage Trick: There are various ways lobbyists can use camouflage techniques to push a point onto the agenda without necessarily divulging the fact that a specific stakeholder is behind it:

  o Cryptic camouflage: Blend in to the point of disappearing, just like a chameleon. Some lobbyists are so close to the people they lobby, that they can get involved in a specific dossier at such an early stage that the outside world is not even aware of their intervention. It is also often a symptom of the revolving doors phenomenon, whereby EU officials become lobbyists and vice versa.

  o Disruptive camouflage: Think of smoke screens or ink clouds from octopuses. The idea is to draw policy-makers' attention to something so eye-catching that they do not notice the real issues at stake. The whole debate between institutions and stakeholders then focuses on this contentious point, allowing a lot of smaller points to 'slip between the cracks', unnoticed.

  o Mimicry: It's about pretending to be someone you are not, just like some flowers mimic the smell and feel of female insects to attract male insects. In lobbying, associations can be used to camouflage your issue as something it is not, a practice which has led to some controversy in the past.[33]

  I personally think that transparency is a must when lobbying but some lobbyists still seem to think these techniques are worth taking the risk of losing one's trust capital.

- The Chimpanzee: Chimps show empathy to other species, going so far as to feed turtles. According to this strategy, a lobbyist tries to act as a dealmaker, by being the one to offer compromises that are acceptable to all involved. This allows the lobbyist to be perceived as 'of good will and reasonable' and even though the 'win' for a client could be less clear cut it can still be more productive than wanting to obtain everything your client can dream of and ending up empty handed. It is also dubbed the 'Kofi Annan' or 'Trojan horse' approach.

---

[33] The Corporate Europe Observatory, a Dutch NGO that monitors lobbyists, criticised for example a PR company in Brussels for having put together an association called the 'Bromine Science and Environment Forum', without making it very explicit that this Forum was created on behalf of the world's four largest bromine producers. See « Brussels – The EU Quarter » by C.E.O., http://archive.corporateeurope.org/docs/lobbycracy/lobbyplanet.pdf

- <u>The Mad Rhino</u>: When they feel under attack, rhinos can become very threatening. Some companies tend to do the same, going from threats of relocation to lawsuits and other niceties, in case a specific piece of legislation or amendment gets adopted. And you know what: if the company is big enough and the threat seems potentially real enough to be taken seriously by policy-makers and politicians, it sometimes works.

- <u>The Tick Bird</u>: For those unfamiliar with tick birds (also referred to as 'Oxpeckers'), they are small birds which remove ticks from rhinos and other large mammals in the African savannahs and Asia. Following this method, you focus first on the juiciest ticks, i.e. on the biggest issues for your client in a piece of legislation, and then only allow yourself to address the more minor issues.

BRUSSELS' APPROACH TO INFORMATION SHARING

Regardless of the strategy adopted, one element remains central: Brussels is a rumour mill where information is power. Getting a leaked document first and choosing whom you share it with are important aspects of EU lobbying. I have dubbed Brussels' approach to transparency and information sharing the 'Calzone syndrome', in reference to the like-named folded pizza which only shows its crust from the outside.

Well, most people in the EU bubble handle information as if it were a calzone:

1. It's better kept hidden for as long as possible;
2. Only two persons in the food chain, in principle, get to see what's inside: the cook that made it, and the client that ordered it. The others just see the crust;
3. The content is a lot more juicier than your mainstream open pizza that's already half dry by the time it reaches your table; and,
4. It's only good if it's hot and fresh. Quoting a pizza manual: "diving into a pale, soggy, undercooked calzone with a filling that is still cold at the center has nothing poetic about it".[34]

---

[34] See http://www.pizzamanual.com/pizza.asp?name=calzone&cat=6&con=0

D. TIMING IS EVERYTHING: BE THERE ON TIME AND ALL THE TIME

MEP assistants often have funny stories of how lobbyists did a poor job trying to influence them and their boss. An assistant once told me how he received a very detailed position paper including amendments on a working document that was internal to the European Commission. In practice, this meant his MEP would not be concerned about this for the next 12 to 18 months (average timing for a European Commission idea to reach the European Parliament) and could not influence until then. For the lobbyist in question, this meant two things: first, his credibility with that MEP was certainly not boosted by his poor timing; secondly, from his client's perspective, the lobbyist did work for nothing by lobbying something at the wrong time (and got paid to do it). I have heard of the reverse happening too, whereby a lobbyist sent MEPs voting recommendation on a piece of legislation, two days after the vote had already taken place.

When it comes to influencing a legislative process, the earlier you get started, the more chances you have of making a significant impact. This is especially true when it comes to removing damaging results from a draft by informing those in charge of the likely outcome of their legislation in practice.

Starting early is especially effective with technical experts writing a document. It is less so with politicians who often have a very short attention span and consider an issue only to be relevant if it is an item featured on the next month's agenda. So in practice, talking to a Commission official who is still busy working on a draft can be extremely effective, whereas lobbying an MEP about an issue not imminently important to them is usually a major waste of time both for you and for them.

Being available all the time does not mean that you can just corner a decision-maker at a cocktail and start hammering your arguments at them. It might however be worth asking them at a social occasion if you can come to their office at some point to discuss a certain issue. More often not, this social approach ends up initiating a discussion on the substance.

Also, make sure that in the positions you draft and advocate, you use up-to-date sources and not a version that was discussed two working groups ago (that happens a lot and is extremely confusing and counterproductive). You should also be extremely careful in reacting to a 'leaked document', i.e. a document that is not yet official but landed on your desk thanks to a friendly soul. Some 'leaked' documents circulate widely and it is a bit of an insider's joke to mention them bluntly. But in certain cases, you can be in possession of an 'exclusive' leak, that maybe the person you are lobbying does not even have sight of. Prudence recommends, when in doubt, to simply talk about 'rumours' and hint at the content of a leaked document without directly quoting or admitting that you have it in your possession.

E.   BE CONCISE AND HELPFUL, SELL YOUR POSITION AND PRIORITISE YOUR 'DEMANDS'

If you cannot summarise your issues on one page and in 15 minutes, you're in deep trouble. Teenagers are not the only ones with an attention span that lasts the time of a video clip: politicians and many non-technical decision makers share that curse as well.

So, whatever medium you use: keep it short, mention the reference and title of the piece of legislation you want to talk about in your papers, tell a story rather than sharing a thesis, and stay on message!

Moreover, when talking to decision-makers, don't talk to them without taking into consideration the specificities of their home country and of their personal background (in other words, you cannot lobby a Romanian engineer from a region suffering rural exodus in the same way as you would approach a British lawyer representing the City in London). If your target is a politician, frame your arguments in such a manner that the benefits for their constituency or the greater good become apparent. Don't just sell your position **to** them, sell it **for** them! In other words, how can helping you also make them help the people they are representing in the Parliament? Bonus question: how could your collaboration be made attractive to the media and the public sphere and translate into an appealing press release).

Finally, ask yourself what you can do for the person you are trying to influence. As they are not necessarily experts in your area, they could consider you a valuable source of information for the future. Offer your assistance, especially on dossiers you do not lobby on but can bring some technical expertise to. Share any information that relates to the views of the other institutions and other major stakeholders lobbying the same dossier. Also, politicians hate to defend a cause without being aware what arguments could be used against them in the process. Preparing your 'champion' against those arguments is therefore essential. 'No surprises' is the golden rule.

F. WILD ANIMALS MEET BY THE WATERING HOLE

If you are serious about lobbying Brussels, you need to get an access badge to the European Parliament. This allows you to enter the Parliament all year around (except when the Parliament is in Strasbourg) and to attend those meetings which focus on the pieces of legislation you are interested in. It is also a good way of meeting not only the MEPs of the relevant Committees but also European Commission staffers who follow the dossier; the representatives of the prevailing Council Presidency; and the representatives from some of the Member States.

Note that getting an EP badge can be somewhat of an ordeal for a lobbyist. You need to prove that you do not have a criminal record; obtain reference letters from previous employers. You should also be prepared to get, on your first application for a badge, a letter from security services stating that something in your initial submission was missing, so that you have to re-start the whole process from scratch. In addition, you have to re-apply for a badge at least every year. Still, the benefits far outweigh the ordeal and once you are a seasoned lobbyist, the process becomes smoother as you can ask MEPs to act as 'references' on the application form.

Remember too that, aside from hanging out at Parliament meetings, Brussels has the highest number of restaurants per capita of any European city, which means the place nurtures a lunch-coffee-meeting culture.

The coffee culture is especially apparent when you visit the bar inside the European Parliament, famously nicknamed the Mickey Mouse cafeteria due to colourful chairs shaped like, well, a giant mouse's ears[35]. Similar to speed dating, you can observe lobbyists meeting one MEP assistant after another (and sometimes even the odd MEP him- or herself) at twenty-minute intervals to discuss dossiers that are particularly 'hot'. If the lobbyists play their cards right, the first date will turn into a second *rendez-vous*.

Moreover, EU officials have their regular watering holes in Brussels and Strasbourg. Seeking them out is therefore not too dissimilar to traditional hunting: if you hang around for long enough at a politician's favourite pub, it is very likely that they will turn up. The same is true for European Commission officials, even if the hang outs are rarely the same.

---

[35] The place kept its name even though it has been fully refurbished in a more 'grown up loungy style', only a couple of the old seats having been kept as a reminder of the origin of the name.

THE GOLDEN RULES FOR A EUROPEAN LOBBYIST

1. <u>Get in early</u>. The earlier you move in, the more you will be able to change things in an effective and substantial manner. Too late means fire-fighting.

2. <u>Be transparent</u>. I do not understand why lobbyists would not divulge who they are representing when talking to others. Does anyone think lobbyists would meet them just on their own, with no one asking them to do so? Transparency also means you should lay out your case and prepare anyone willing to support against all the counter-argument they may face. Finally, transparency implies that, if making your arguments attractive is a must, spinning and sins of omission should be avoided.

3. <u>Put yourself in their shoes and propose solutions.</u> Explain things from your target's perspective and tell them how they can help, including by having the properly drafted amendments ready for them.

4. <u>Monitor, monitor, monitor</u>. The EU is a very political environment and new issues never cease to pop up. Even when you think you solved a problem, never let your guard down until the measure is adopted and can no longer be changed by last minute horse trading. Information is power in Brussels.

5. <u>Building a network is pointless if you do not maintain it.</u> All institutions matter and building a network is a never-ending enterprise. Try to regularly get in touch with civil servants and MEP assistants and ask them if they want to grab a coffee or a quick lunch, especially when you have nothing to ask from them.

6. <u>Be critical and tough on your clients</u> to ensure that they identify all the right issues. Asking for too much is pointless, but missing important issues at the start of a process makes it so much more difficult to address them later on.

7. <u>Manage client expectations</u>. Aim at the moon but be prepared (and prepare your client) to settle for a star. It is the follow-up to the previous rule: Brussels is about managing the nuances of gray. In terms of end results, Europe doesn't do white, tries to avoid black, but excels at discovering the multiple facets of gray.

8. <u>Know your stuff</u>. Do not accept to go into meetings only half prepared or with a client that only tells you half of the story. Talk to the company you represent, play devil's advocate, challenge and quiz them until you feel absolutely comfortable that you are fully briefed and that you believe in your message.

9. <u>Keep it short and simple</u> with politicians. Simple and clear messages work best, with the underlying detailed arguments to show that you did your homework and that each of your messages relies on sound facts and evidence.

10. <u>Be accessible</u>. There is a reason why I hand out my mobile number on my business card and do not use a personal assistant: missing one call at a critical moment can create irredeemable damage.

CHAP. 3: WHEN? –LEGISLATIVE PROCEDURES AND PROPER TIMING

I. INTRODUCTION

The EU legislative process follows a series of steps, some of which occur a long time before any official proposal of legislation emerges on the public scene, and some of which happen in parallel to the official steps taken by each legislative instrument.

In order to ensure that you adopt the most effective strategy, it is therefore critical to understand and master the EU legislative process. It is part of your 3Ps (People-Power-Procedures) and I have known several brilliant lobbying strategies failing because the intricacies of procedure were poorly addressed.

The key message is obvious: the earlier you get in, the more likely you are to make a difference. On the other hand, lobbying is often like a poker party: by showing your hand too early, you allow other stakeholders that disagree with you to fight back for a longer time. Changes to a legislative text that occur early in the process also need to be defended very carefully until the discussed legislative proposal is adopted. Losing a sentence that matters to you in a piece of legislation because of sloppy transcripts from one version of a document to another, or because no one really thought that sentence was important, or the fact that other interested stakeholders effectively campaigned against it, etc., all of that can still happen and the earlier your amendments gets in, the longer you need to be very watchful that they stay in.

Moreover, if you handled a dossier "on the fly" (i.e. a client comes to you when a proposal has already been put forward by the European Commission and is at a more or less advance stage of its adoption), knowing at what stage you are in a process is key to assess what can be realistically achieved and who needs to be made aware of your issue and its possible solution.

In this chapter, we examine the different legislative procedures in place at EU level, and how the decision-making process can be influenced, from the moment an EU instrument is being conceived as an idea, to the moment it is adopted as EU law and then transposed into the national law of each Member State.

II. LEGISLATIVE PROCEDURE

BUSINESSES EXPECT SPEED WHEN THE EU MOVES AT THE PACE OF A SNAIL

A legislative procedure can take up to three years from the moment an idea originated until the adoption of a text. This is extremely long and often unsettling for businesses which work according to a quarterly reporting logic and are used to immediate results. As a result, companies either:

Procrastinate on a certain dossier and thus completely ignore the procedural limitations in terms of amending a text at a late stage and will be forced to do damage control instead of proactively influencing proceedings; or,
Get discouraged or sloppy during the process and let things fall between the cracks.

It is indeed difficult to stay alert throughout the entire process when the same text is being amended in different institutions at the same time. In some cases, when faced with too many amendments, one has to prioritise which parts of the text need to be scrutinised, and hope that other stakeholders look at the rest with equally watchful eyes. But the fact that so many different stakeholders are looking at the same texts as you are, can have its positive and negative sides. On the positive, there is a certain amount of 'free riding' to be done when it comes to trusting that stakeholders with a similar interest as the company you represent will cover some issues you do not have the time to address. On the negative side, knowing that stakeholders that oppose the views you are also lobbying, it is often safer to ensure certain amendments that matter to the company you defend are inserted in very differing parts of a Directive or package of Directives: this can in some cases mean that, if stakeholders with opposed interests are too focused on one place, they could miss the changes you got slipped in elsewhere.

Talking to stakeholders from different camps is always a good way to get a broader picture of a piece of legislation. You might be interested in one particular issue, but larger associations or companies are likely to follow a variety of issues and can therefore provide you with valuable insight into the broader picture. Remember that patience and persistence pay off in the end.

A. General description

The legislative process extends well beyond the three-step boogie danced during co-decision or one of the other legislative adoption processes of the EU institutions.

Months pass before a proposal is sent to the Parliament and Council for discussions. Like a good bottle of wine, this allows the content to mature and develop at its own pace. The 'early idea' stage also represents a perfect opportunity for lobbyists to influence the process more efficiently.

Conversely, after certain legislative instruments such as Directives are adopted, they still need to be 'transposed' into national law. This often requires a fair bit of work to avoid national legislators making creative interpretations of the texts adopted in Brussels when translating them into national law, especially when such interpretations could have damaging consequences. On the other hand, in certain cases, creative interpretations can be encouraged to get a better result at national level than what was achievable at EU level.

Roughly summarised, the legislative procedure undergoes the following steps (see Figure 7): idea, draft, proposal, EU law and transposition into national law.

FIGURE 7-THE STEPS FOLLOWED BY EU LEGISLATION

Each of these steps involves different EU institutions and players, which makes it sometimes difficult to focus and build the most efficient influencing strategy, especially if you do not have your ears on the ground in Brussels due to a permanent presence.

B. Idea

The earlier you start lobbying a legislative measure, the more chances you stand to influence it significantly. In fact, initiating the idea of a legislative measure is even more likely to help you obtain the wished result. This does require continuous monitoring and interaction with all three institutions all along the legislative process, to avoid your brilliant suggestion being turned into a piece of legislation that at best, does not help your client and, at worst, actually back fires against him.

It is also important for lobbyists to spot ideas emerging in a legislator's mind at a very early stage. This requires decrypting a lot of documents and public interventions (e.g. speeches by Commissioners), some of which are listed in this section. It also means having a lot of informal chats with European Commission officials, both at DG and Cabinet levels.

1.   EUROPEAN COMMISSION INITIATIVES

POLICY STRATEGY AND WORK PROGRAMME

The Commission's work programme and strategic vision is planned and reported in different documents, namely:

- 5-year plan: The Commission establishes a five-year strategic objective, which is used as guidance over the duration of its term of office[36]. This plan can be influenced notably by introducing certain issues during the interview and screening Commissioners undergo in the European Parliament before being appointed. If an MEP asks a Commissioner what their view is on a given issue, the answer is 'on the record' and lobbyists often quote these statements back at the Cabinet staff of that Commissioner.
- Commission Annual Policy Strategy: This strategy is outlined during an orientation debate held amongst the College of Commissioners. The Secretary-General then communicates the results to the services (DGs and other services such as legal, translation, etc.) who in turn draft subsequent proposals. Once adopted, each part of the Annual Policy Strategy is presented by the Commissioner in charge to the relevant EP Committees and Council configurations. The outcome is used to prepare the Commission's work programme for the following year.
- Directorate-General Annual Management Plan: Based on the Commission's plan, each DG then develops its annual management plan.

---

[36] This plan can also set goals and objectives which extend well beyond the five-year term of the Commission and Parliament, as is the case at present with the EU2020 due to replace the Lisbon Strategy and cover the period 2010-2020.

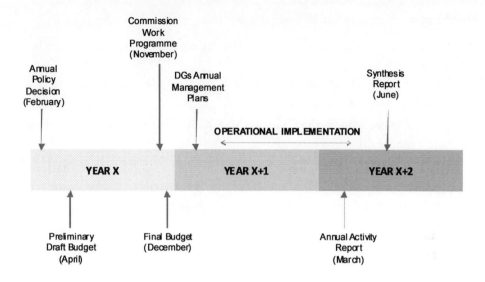

FIGURE 8-EUROPEAN COMMISSION'S STRATEGIC PLANNING AND PROGRAMMING CYCLE

Though all of these documents are written in a very high level way, it can be interesting to try to get what lobbyists call 'hooks' in them. These are basically references to action items or priorities, written in a sufficiently general manner that they do not raise the attention (internally within the Commission and externally with other stakeholders not sharing your views). Once these 'hooks' are in place, lobbyists will quote them to Cabinet and DG officials of the European Commission to try and obtain a legislative improvement. This has been for example the case in 2010 with the lobbying of the EU 2020 strategy set out by the Barroso II Commission.

CONSULTATIVE DOCUMENTS

Prior to proposing any form of legislation, the Commission usually holds a round of consultations to get input from all concerned stakeholders. These consultations are usually posted on individual DG websites, but a complete list can be found at http://ec.europa.eu/yourvoice/consultations/index_en.htm .

Importantly, the Commission can also issue two types of pre-proposal papers to test the opinions of stakeholders on certain topics:

- <u>Green Papers</u>, which are aimed at stimulating the debate on a particular issue; and,
- <u>White Papers</u>, which are often the follow-up of a Green Paper, set out concrete proposals for action by the Commission in a specific area. When favourably received by the Council, these White Papers can then be turned into a proper EU action programme.

Lobbyists respond to such Papers the same way they respond to consultations (and both processes are often combined by the Commission, by issuing a consultation on the Green Paper, in order to include the feedback of comments in the White Paper).

EXPERT GROUPS

Membership to so-called Expert Groups is a very important move in most sectors for any company wishing to have its views communicated at all stages of the policy process. Some of the focus areas, in which these groups intervene, include the setting of targets for air quality, authorising cosmetic products, establishing automobile safety standards, determining sustainable fish catches, developing strategies to tackle unemployment or public health concerns, or designing European research programmes.

The European Commission tends to consult more and more such Expert Groups, prior to drafting and implementing European laws and policies. These advisory groups can be temporary or permanent, and are made up of national and/or private sector experts (e.g. national officials, scientists, academics, but also representatives of trade associations, companies, consumer groups, NGOs, civil society organisations, etc.).

Their advice can intervene at different stages of the policy process:

- <u>Development phase</u>: Experts Groups can either identify an area requiring the Commission's intervention or provide advice regarding the drafting of a legislative proposal, including the impact assessment, which outlines how a piece of legislation affects citizens and industry, as well as the economy;

- <u>Implementing phase</u>: Expert Groups can also assist the Commission when it drafts implementing measures, prior to their submission to a Comitology committee[37]; and,
- <u>Monitoring and evaluation phase</u>: Expert Groups also assist the Commission in evaluating the implementation of acts and their enforcement by relevant national authorities.

Statistics show that since 2000, the total number of these Expert Groups has increased by more than 40 percent, the total number of Expert Group members currently exceeding 50,000.

Industry is highly represented in Expert Groups covering enterprise, agriculture and research. However, more than 50 percent of Expert Groups only include government experts and national officials, representatives of industry or NGOs being excluded.

SURVIVAL TIP

Expert groups are interesting at two levels: (1) they allow you to influence the thinking process at an extremely early stage of its development and (2) they allow industry representatives to create informal ties with officials from both the European institutions and national governments.

OTHER

There are numerous other places that let you gauge the Commission's opinion: speeches by Commissioners or Director Generals, hearings, workshops, conferences and seminars. Particularly valuable is the list of tenders for studies by external consultants. Not always easy to track, it can often be found on DG's individual websites.

---

[37] Comitology Committees are forums of discussion bringing together representatives from Member States and the European Commission (chair) and aimed assisting the Commission in implementing EU laws. Each EU law indicates if a Comitology Committee should intervene in its implementation, and which form of comitology committee should be set up. The European Parliament is allowed to verify what these Committees do in some cases.

2. COUNCIL INITIATIVES

PRIORITIES OF THE PRESIDENCY

Every six months, the rotating Presidency of the Council issues so-called Priorities for its tenure. This is complemented since two years with an 18-months plan, which needs to be agreed upon by the three successive Presidencies[38] to ensure the consistency and coherence of the Council Work Programme.

CONCLUSIONS OF THE EUROPEAN COUNCIL

The European Council's role is defined as "giving the European Union the necessary impetus for the Union's development and defining EU general political guidelines, in particular in the field of Common Foreign and Security Policy (CFSP)".

The European Council is not a formal law-making body as such but the European Union's leading decision-making body, with sensitive issues being discussed and settled at European Council meetings.

The agreements made by the Heads of State and Government are reached by consensus, not by voting. They are made public in the form of Presidency Conclusions which define political guidelines for the EU institutions.

These conclusions are important because they explain the policy direction the Council wishes to take on a certain issue. However, because they are usually short and try to express a consensus rather quickly reached between the 27 Member States, they tend to translate into rather fluffy and superficial documents. As a result, lobbyists will typically extract the one sentence that they believe serves their interest and quote it out of context whenever appropriate.

---

[38] See page 14 regarding the so-called 'Troika or Trio concept'.

Council Conclusions should not however be used in all circumstances, as European Commission civil servants tend to be quite dismissive about them. I witnessed once how the representative of a trade association quoted Spring Council conclusions during a meeting with people from DG Competition, which prompted a rather dry reply that "Council conclusions have no legal value", sending a definite chill over the rest of the meeting. It is therefore better to use Council text with national governments and Council representatives, and to be more cautious in using them when lobbying the European Commission and EP.

3.   EUROPEAN PARLIAMENT INITIATIVES

RESOLUTIONS OF THE EUROPEAN PARLIAMENT ON ANNUAL STRATEGY

The European Commission must present its Annual Policy Strategy to the EP, which in turn issues a Resolution commenting on it. This document highlights the areas the Parliament would like the Commission to focus on, but also indicates its disagreement with certain points of the proposed plan.

PARLIAMENTARY QUESTIONS

Parliamentary Questions have the merit of forcing the Commission or the Council to provide an answer that is 'on the record'. That is why they are often used by lobbyists (suggesting them to MEPs) to 'get a feel' in a rather informal way on how the Commission feels about a certain issue.

The Parliament can use three types of questions:

- Questions for oral answer with debate: These questions can be tabled by a committee, a political group or a minimum of 40 MEPs. The Conference of Presidents decides whether, and in what order questions are placed on the agenda and the questions must be communicated to the Council or the Commission at least one week before the sitting.

- Oral questions for Question Time: MEPs can put only one question to the Council and Commission at a given part-session, and these questions must be submitted in writing to the President of the Parliament.
  The procedure differs slightly depending on the questioned institution:

- o For the Council, questions are called in the chronological order in which they have been tabled; and,
- o For the Commission, question time is divided into three parts, namely (1) topical political matters; (2) questions to the specific Commissioners designated for the part-session and (3) other questions.

Oral questions have to be well-written and short, as MEPs only have one minute to read them.

- <u>Written questions:</u> Questions for written answers may be issued by any MEP to the Council or Commission, but must be transferred to these institutions by the President of the Parliament. The deadline for Commission or Council to respond is six weeks for non-priority questions and three weeks for priority questions. MEPs are allowed to table only one priority question per month, and the President is the final judge.

The list of Parliamentary Questions can be found on the EP's website at http://www.europarl.europa.eu/QP-WEB/home.jsp?language=en .

WRITTEN DECLARATIONS

MEPs can also table a written declaration, which basically is a short statement (no more than 200 words) on any policy area that falls within the scope of activities of the EU. This declaration is included in a specific register and every MEP can add their signature to the declaration. If, after three months, the absolute majority of MEPs have not signed up the declaration, it lapses.

However, if such an absolute majority has been reached, the declaration is notified at plenary (including the names of the signatories), included in the minutes, and communicated to the relevant institutions. It is basically a pressure tool used by MEPs to force the other institutions into action or express their discontent.

WHEN EP WRITTEN DECLARATIONS STIR UP CONTROVERSY

Written declarations can sometimes be used in a misleading manner. For example, in 2010, a Written Declaration (referred to as 'Written Declaration 29' or 'WD 29') circulated with the stated objective to request more to be done to fight against Children being abused. A flurry of MEPs signed this Declaration, the stated objective being difficult not to agree with. However, in doing so without reading the text in great detail, MEPs did not notice that this declaration included a measures pushing for Internet blocking, censorship and retention of personal data. When activists starting alerting them of this fact, some MEPs withdrew their signature but a majority refused to admit that they had signed the document without truly understanding its implications. It is not yet certain that 'WD 29' will reach absolute majority, but the campaign around it was so well orchestrated (specific website allocated to it with very poignant pictures of scared children, posters in the EP Brussels and Strasbourg offices at every elevator asking MEPs to sign, etc.) that it is rumoured that industry lobbyists are behind it.

OWN-INITIATIVE REPORTS

In the areas where the treaties give the EP the right of initiative, its committees may draw up a report on a subject within its remit and present a motion for a resolution to Parliament. They must request authorisation from the Conference of Presidents before drawing up a report.

SURVIVAL TIP

Non legislative instruments such as own initiative reports have specific rules as regards amendments. The Rapporteur is very limited in terms of length of the Report they present to other MEPs. In turn, MEPs can propose as many amendments as they want, but these amendments can only cover the motion itself, not the Explanatory Statements attached to it (this statements forms the justification of the motion and sets out the justifications of the motion recommendations). Getting an early draft directly from the Rapporteur is therefore critical, if you want to impact the entire document.

C. Draft: the role of Inter-service Consultation

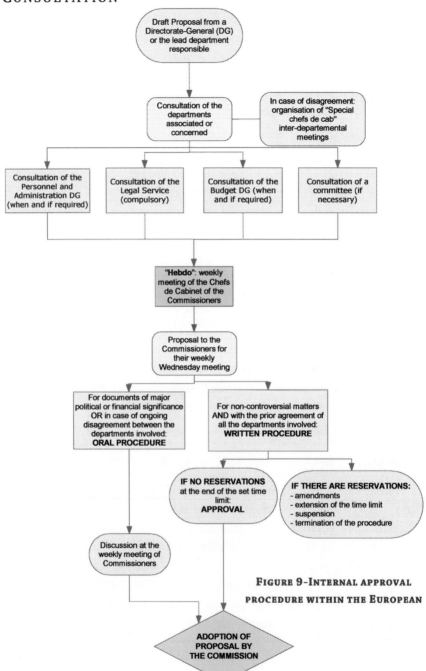

FIGURE 9-INTERNAL APPROVAL
PROCEDURE WITHIN THE EUROPEAN

1.   GENERAL DESCRIPTION

Inter-service consultation occurs within the European Commission at every step of the adoption of a legislative measure, i.e. before a draft legislation is officially put forward by the Commission but also at later stages if the Commission amends its proposal for example in the framework of a co-decision procedure.

At draft stage, inter-service consultation is initiated by the lead DG when a proposal has reached a sufficiently advanced stage within the service, possibly with other services which have been involved from the outset. For example, in the case of Directives relating to the regulation of electronic communications, both the Information Society and Media Directorate-General and the Competition Directorate-General are involved, as 'co-leads', with many other DGs consulted.

When a dossier is complex or sensitive, lead departments often first have informal contacts with the other services that could be affected, either through inter-departmental meetings or bilateral contacts.

For a lobbyist, inter-service consultation is often a manner to achieve changes at a very early stage in the process, and in a rather discreet manner. Moreover, because it is a process that is internal to the Commission, the lead DG and Commissioner is often more receptive to suggested changes coming from other Commissioners (or in practice, their cabinets) than they are to changes coming from the EP or the Council.

It does require quite some stamina as lobbyists must often try to meet a dozen different members of Cabinet within a week's time to convince at least one (but usually two to three) to 'stick their neck out' and intervene in an inter-service consultation process.

2.   SPECIFIC ASPECTS

WHO IS CONSULTED?

The lead department must send its draft document and request the formal opinion of all the DGs and services that have a legitimate interest in the content of a proposal, taking into account the often conflicting objectives of transparency and efficiency.

The Legal Services must always be consulted, while the Secretariat-General and the Personnel and Administration DG, Budget DG and OLAF[39] have to be consulted only when they are specifically affected.

TIME LIMIT FOR REACTION

Inter-service consultations can happen quickly as the minimum initial time limit for DGs to give their comments to the lead DG is 10 or 15 working days, the latter applying for any document longer than 20 pages (annexes excluded). The lead DG may however decide to accept replies that have been submitted late.

SURVIVAL TIP

Because of the speed at which inter-service consultations occur, it is best to keep a network of all Cabinet members in charge of the portfolio items you follow, and to manage it on a constant basis. This requires hard work, as the average lifetime of a Cabinet member is two years and a half, after which quite a few of them join a DG or leave the Commission alltogether. But the good news is that the cafeteria in the Berlaymont building (where all Commissioners and Cabinets are vested) has very good Italian coffee referred to, by insiders as, "un petit / grand Illy".

POSSIBLE REACTIONS OF OTHER SERVICES

Five options are available to the consulted services individually:

- No observations;
- Approval;
- Approval subject to comments or amendments being taken into account;
- Unfavourable opinion - quite a drastic step bound to be met with revenge from the 'vetoed' service during a following inter-service consultation initiated by the 'vetoing' DG; and,
- Suspended opinion, which must be duly substantiated (e.g. insufficient time or lack of essential information) as it freezes the process for technical reasons.

---

[39] OLAF is the European Anti-Fraud Office and is the abbreviation of its French name (Office de Lutte Anti-Fraude).

Once the consultation period has ended, the lead DG must revise the text, trying to take into consideration the comments received. If it chooses to disregard some of the suggestions, it must explain in writing to the services concerned why it has chosen to ignore certain of their annotations.

If the redrafted text is substantially different from the initial proposal, the consultation must be re-launched or extended by a minimum of three working days, and all the services concerned must be duly informed.

In case of dispute between the lead department and a consulted department, the Secretariat-General can be asked to intervene as an arbitrator.

ADOPTION BY THE COLLEGE OF COMMISSIONERS

Depending on the degree of opposition voiced during inter-service consultation, the draft can become an official Commission proposal according to different procedures:

- The <u>oral</u> procedure is used for controversial or politically sensitive files which require a debate within the College of Commissioners during their Wednesday meetings. This only covers a small percentage of proposals (less than 10 percent compared to the total of written procedures). Most of the oral procedure decisions are in the fields of Economic and Financial Affairs, and Competition.

- The <u>written</u> procedure, normally reserved for uncontroversial dossiers, is sometimes used to try and slip a dossier through without it ever reaching the radar screen of Commissioners. In this case, it is often a test of concentration on the Chef de Cabs (and guts) for them to then request that the text go through oral procedure (which is a form of 'political escalation'). Because so many files go through written procedure (about 3,000 per year), cabinets do not always spot that a dossier is more controversial than its title could indicate. It is often lobbyists that bring such draft proposals to their attention by asking them to step in and intervene. This is necessary as, under the written procedure, the file is deemed adopted if none of the consulted services has any reservations before the deadline. The written procedure is mainly used in fields like Health and Consumer Protection, Agriculture, External aid and Enterprise.

- The <u>empowerment</u> procedure concerns clearly defined management and administrative acts, for which a single or several Commissioners receive a mandate by the full College to take measures in its name and under its responsibility, within strict limits and conditions. Over 2,000 dossiers were adopted this way in 2009, mostly in the field of Competition, Regional policy and Agriculture. It is mostly an internal procedure tool and not one that is relevant to lobbyists.

- The <u>delegation</u> procedure, whereby, for a specific technical matter, the College of Commissioners gives a mandate to a Director General or Head of Service to act in its name but in such a defined and narrow manner that they do not have any margin of manoeuvre. This has become de facto the most used internal decision-making method of the Commission, with nearly 4,500 dossiers handled in this manner in 2009.

D. PROPOSAL: THE DIFFERENT LEGISLATIVE PROCEDURES

1. INTRODUCTION

There are four main types of legislative procedures at EU level:

- Ordinary Legislative Procedure (known as Co-decision prior to the entry into force of the Lisbon Treaty and still referred to under that term by most if not all Brussels lobbyists and EU institution officials, which is why this book still uses the co-decision term for convenience);
- Consent (known as Assent prior to the Lisbon Treaty);
- Co-operation; and
- Consultation.

The Treaty defines which procedure should be followed depending mainly on the area covered by a legislative proposal.

In this Chapter, we will mainly concentrate on the co-decision procedure, as it is the most common one.

2.   CO-DECISION PROCEDURE

Prior to the Lisbon Treaty, the co-decision procedure applied to nearly 70 percent of the legislative procedures, basically covering all of the areas requiring at least a qualified majority in the Council with the exception of the Common Agricultural, and Commercial Policies.

However, it did not apply to several important areas like Fiscal Policy for instance, which require unanimity in the Council.

With entry into force of the Lisbon Treaty, co-decision now covers 40 additional areas (making it a total of 83 areas) and is therefore considered as the 'ordinary legislative procedure', as opposed to the 'special legislative procedures'.

Documents that must undergo co-decision are marked with the code "COD".

SURVIVAL TIP

As a lobbyist, you must be prepared (and prepare your client) to the fact that co-decision usually plays out best for those that have the patience and perseverance required to make the most of the length and complexity of the procedure. There are multiple steps involving each of the three EU institutions. Some would consider this a nightmare but a seasoned lobbyist knows that if each step represents a possible risk (of either losing pieces of legislative text that you liked or seeing things creep in you dislike) it also implies a new chance to insert one's issue.

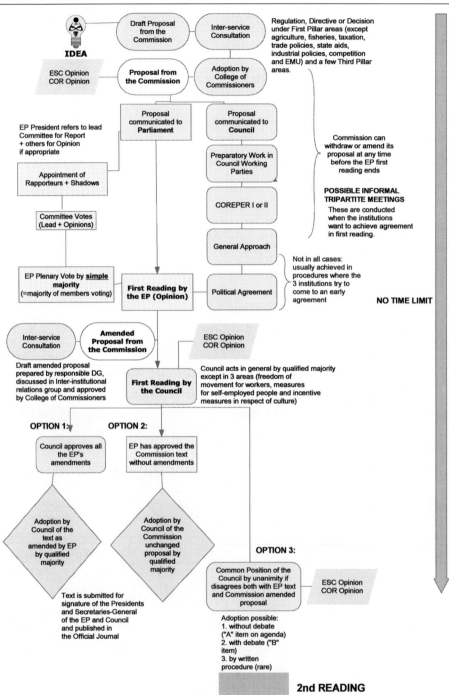

FIGURE 10-CO-DECISION IN 1ST READING

(I) STEP 1: COMMISSION PROPOSAL

Under Co-decision, the Commission has the right of initiative and issues a proposal, which is sent to the European Parliament and the Council, both institutions working in parallel to analyse and amend this proposal.

Note that both the Commission and the Council must consult the European Economic and Social Committee (ESC) and the Committee of Regions (CoR), if the Treaty requires it or if the Commission and Council deem it to be an appropriate move. Moreover, the ESC and CoR can issue an opinion at their own initiative, or at a request of the EP.

In such cases, the Council or the Commission can set time limits for the submission of opinions in order to avoid unnecessary delays.

(II) STEP 2: EP FIRST READING

(A) TIME LIMITS

The EP delivers an Opinion at first reading. Although there is no official time limit, this phase normally lasts about eight months, unless the dossier is of complex technical or political nature.

(B) ADOPTION AT EP COMMITTEE LEVEL

The Opinion is prepared at two levels:

- At Parliamentary Committee level
- At Plenary level.

When the Commission text reaches the EP, the Parliamentary Committee responsible is named (known as the lead Committee), along with any other Committees which are asked for an opinion.

Within the lead Committee, the Political Groups' coordinators designate a Rapporteur entrusted with the drafting of the Report containing the proposed amendments put forward by the EP. Other Political Groups may also appoint a

Shadow Rapporteur responsible for preparing the Group's position and monitoring the work of the Rapporteur[40].

The Parliamentary Committee meets several times to study the draft report prepared by the Rapporteur and the amendments put forward by other MEPs. All amendments (i.e. those from the lead Committee and all other Committees asked for an Opinion) are put to vote in the Parliamentary Committee responsible, on the basis of a simple majority.

(C) ADOPTION IN EP PLENARY

Once the report is adopted at Committee level, it goes to plenary. Additional amendments to the report, including amendments adopted in the Parliamentary Committee, may be tabled by Political Groups or at least 40 MEPs and put to a plenary vote.

As a general rule, the deadline for tabling new amendments at this stage is noon on the Thursday of the week preceding the plenary session.

In practice, this means that if an MEP wants to table an amendment at plenary and does not have the support of his political group, he will have to find 39 other MEPs willing to sign his amendment. This is done on paper, and requires a poor assistant running from one office to another to physically collect the signatures of MEPs that are willing and present. It is not rare for such an exercise to fail, not necessarily because the amendment did not have enough support, but because it was physically impossible for the assistant to find 39 MEPs in their office before the deadline for tabling the amendment. It is also not a done thing for lobbyists to assist such a process by helping in the collection of signatures, although it does happen that lobbyists phone up MEPs to ask them to sign the amendment of their colleague MEP.

Plenary sessions follow a set script with strict limits on speaking times. Ahead of the vote, the Rapporteurs and Shadow Rapporteurs present their Report, followed by the relevant Commissioner. The Commissioner's reaction is written by his or her Directorate-General and must be approved by the College of Commissioners (following discussions between cabinets in the Inter-institutional relations group[41]).

---

[40] See page 50.
[41] See page 33 as regards the role of Cabinets.

In first reading, a simple majority (i.e. majority of MEPs present during the vote) is required to adopt the EP amendments, either on an amendment-by-amendment basis or as a whole block. The latter occurs when the report has been adopted in Parliamentary Committee with a 90-percent majority and the Rapporteur requested that the Report be voted on during plenary without further amendment or debate.

(III) STEP 3: COMMISSION AMENDED PROPOSAL

Following the EP's first reading vote, the Commission usually issues a so-called Amended Proposal, which sets out its views on the amendments adopted by the EP, often in three sections[42]:

- Amendments accepted by the Commission (presented simply as a list of numbers referring to the numbering of the adopted report in Parliament);
- Amendments accepted by the Commission subject to re-drafting. The re-drafting requested by the Commission is included in the Amended Proposal; and,
- Amendments rejected by the Commission (also presented as a list of numbers referring to the numbering of the adopted EP Report).

The Amended Proposal is prepared by the Commission's DG in charge of the dossier, on the basis of the mandate obtained from the College of Commissioners before the plenary. The Legal Service and the Secretariat-General are consulted, and the Amended Proposal is adopted by the College and published in the Official Journal.

(IV) STEP 4: COUNCIL FIRST READING

The Council examines the Commission's initial proposal in parallel to the EP.

This work is conducted within specific working groups[43]. These working groups are chaired by the Member State holding the rotating Council Presidency, and comprise representatives of each Member State. They are assisted in their work by the General Secretariat of the Council. The Commission attends these meetings and is supposed to provide expert advice.

---

[42] See Annex 6 on page 205 for an example of Amended Proposal layout.
[43] See page 21 where we examine these working groups in detail.

The work done in the working groups is then presented to the Coreper (I or II), which prepares every Council of Ministers decision. Decisions prepared by Coreper are adopted by the Council of Ministers either without debate, when an agreement has been found at the preparatory stage (A item), or with debate (B item)[44].

(D) POSSIBLE INTERMEDIATE STEPS

Prior to reaching a Common Position, Council can adopt two intermediate steps:

- The Council may, on occasion, reach an agreement in principle before the EP delivers its opinion. This early agreement by the Council is referred to as a 'general approach'. This is not a common occurrence and is mainly used in cases where there is a strong impetus to reach a first-reading agreement; or,
- More often, the Council first reaches a political agreement laying down the broad outlines of the proposed common position. The details of this agreement are subsequently finalised by the working group, verified by lawyer-linguists and formally adopted as a Common Position by the Council of Ministers at a subsequent meeting.

Because the Council and EP review run at the same time, the Council normally only finalises formally its Position once it knows what the EP's first reading amendments are and what the Commission's resulting amended proposal is.

(E) AVAILABLE SCENARIOS

There are different scenarios possible, but in the areas of culture, freedom of movement, social security and coordination of the rules for carrying out a profession, the Council always needs to reach unanimity (abstentions do not count as a negative vote).

In all other areas, there are three possible scenarios:

- If the EP has not adopted any amendments to the Commission's proposal and the Council accepts without alteration the Commission's proposal, the act can be adopted by qualified majority.
- If the Council does not introduce any amendments and accepts all the amendments adopted by the European Parliament, the act can be adopted by qualified majority.

---

[44] See page 18 for a detailed overview of this terminology.

In both this case and the scenario set out above, the outcome is an early first-reading-agreement. The legislative act is then submitted directly for the signature of the Presidents and Secretaries-General of the European Parliament and of the Council, and is published in the Official Journal, ending the procedure.

- If the Council introduces amendments to the European Parliament adopted text, two sub-options are possible:

    (1) If the Council's Position is in line with the Commission's amended proposal, it can adopt its Common Position by qualified majority; or,

    (2) If the Council position is not in line with the Commission's amended proposal, then unanimity is required to adopt its Common Position. In this case, there will be a <u>second reading</u>. The Council's Common Position is forwarded to the EP together with a so-called Statement of reasons[45] usually at the plenary session following its formal adoption. The time limits laid down by the Treaty for the subsequent stages of the procedure start to run when the EP receives the common position[46].

(F) TIME LIMITS

There is no time limit laid down in the Treaty for the adoption of a Common Position by the Council. On average, this phase lasts roughly 15 months, depending on the complexity of the dossiers. The adoption of certain politically sensitive common positions has, however, taken several years in some cases!

(G) INFORMAL TRIALOGUES

When co-legislators are seeking to conclude an agreement at first reading, they often organise informal tripartite meetings attended by representatives of:

- The EP (Rapporteur and, where appropriate, Shadow Rapporteurs);
- The Council (chair of the working group and/or Coreper); and,
- The European Commission (DG(s) responsible for the dossier and the Commission's Secretariat-General), acting as mediator and technical support.

The aim is to ensure that the EP amendments adopted in the plenary session are acceptable to the Council.

---

[45] All of which must be translated into the 23 official and working languages.
[46] Or more precisely on the day following this formal receipt.

THE GOLDEN RULES IN FIRST READING

1. Make sure all the amendments that need to be tabled are tabled by an MEP. Rules for tabling amendments in second reading are a lot more stringent so missing the boat in first reading is usually fatal.

2. Find more than one MEP willing to support you, and try to avoid having different MEPs tabling exactly the same amendment. They are often irritated when that happens as it makes it obvious that the amendment was not drafted by them. Moreover, should two MEPs from Political Groups with very diverging opinions table the exact same text, they could face some embarrassment internally (and obviously make you pay for it).

3. Be prepared to hand over draft amendments in different languages. MEPs usually prefer to table texts in their native language as it looks less conspicuous.

4. Focus first on the Rapporteur, then on the Shadows and the Coordinators. If all else fails, find other MEPs to either simply table your amendment for procedure's sake or – preferred option – table and actively defend your issue.

5. Don't forget to brief the Commission and Council about the amendments that have been tabled in the EP thanks to you (and the amendments you are trying to get killed by lobbying for a negative vote against them). If you do not brief them, they may not understand what the objective of your amendment is, as the justifications below them are often quite cryptic. Do not say however the amendment might have been initiated by you: just say it is spot on (or dead wrong) for your client, and why.

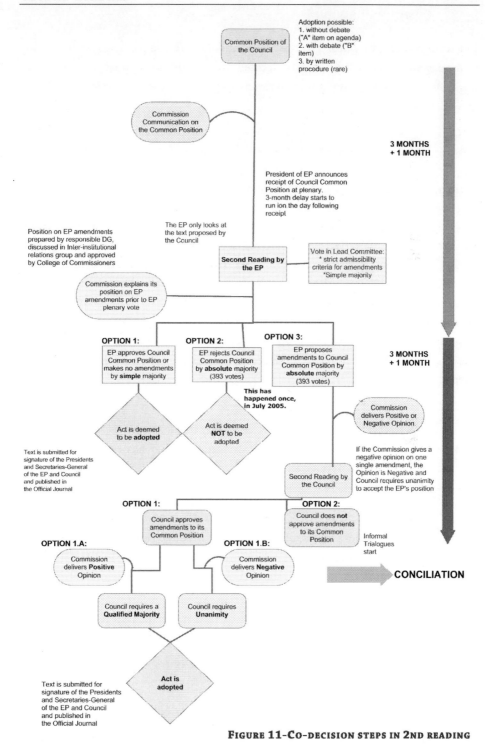

FIGURE 11-CO-DECISION STEPS IN 2ND READING

(I) STEP 5: COMMISSION COMMUNICATION ON THE COUNCIL COMMON POSITION

In this document, forwarded to the EP in tandem with the common position, the Commission explains why it has decided to support or oppose the common position reached by Council and comments on the Council's reaction to the EP amendments.

(II) STEP 6: EP SECOND READING

Compared to the first reading, the second reading is much stricter as regards both the timing, the type of amendments that can be put forward and the majority threshold that needs to be reached in EP plenary. These elements are important to take into consideration when putting together a lobbying strategy, as they mean that second reading is a bad place to introduce 'new ideas': first, MEPs have less time to understand them than in first reading; secondly, MEPs are very limited in the type of amendments they can table (see infra). Lobbyists must therefore make sure that all the changes they want to see introduced are tabled as amendments at first reading (and thus ensure the companies they represent thoroughly analyse everything they need to avoid procedure being held against them).

(A) TIME LIMITS

The EP has three months (with a possible one-month extension) to take action on the basis of the Council's common position.

(B) AMENDMENT LIMITATIONS

The adoption procedure at second reading is broadly similar to that at first reading, but with substantial restrictions regarding the nature of the amendments, which can only be tabled if they comply with one or more of the following criteria:

- The amendments must aim to restore wholly or partly an amendment adopted at first reading and not accepted by the Council;
- The amendments must concern a part of the common position, which did not appear in, or is substantially different from, the Commission's initial proposal;

- The amendments must introduce a compromise between the positions of the co-legislators; or,
- The amendments must take into account a new fact or legal situation, which has arisen since the first reading.

(c) ADOPTION AT EP COMMITTEE LEVEL

The procedure for second reading in parliamentary committee generally follows the rules and practice of the first reading, with the difference that the text to be amended is the Council's common position and not the Commission's proposal.

Normally, only the lead Committee is involved (but there are exceptions where other Committees can also intervene).

The amendments adopted in the Parliamentary committee form the so-called 'Recommendation for second reading', which is normally defended by the same Rapporteur as at the first reading. Amendments may also be tabled personally by other MEPs.

The proposed amendments are put to the vote in the Parliamentary Committee, which takes a decision by simple majority.

(d) ADOPTION IN PLENARY:

Only Political Groups or 40 MEPs can table additional amendments at the EP plenary.

The EP plenary adopts amendments by absolute majority (and not simple majority as is the case in first reading), meaning that a majority of the <u>total</u> number of MEPs must approve.

Different scenarios can occur:

- If the EP, (1) approves the Council Common position without amendments; (2) does not take a decision within the time limit; (3) or is unable to reach the absolute majority required to adopt tabled amendments, the EP President will declare that the Common Position is approved.
- If the EP rejects the Common Position by an absolute majority, the act is deemed to not have been adopted and the procedure ends. It must be noted that this right to simply reject the Council's Common Position has never been used in practice by the Parliament.

- If the EP proposes amendments to the Common Position and obtains the required absolute majority, the amended text is forwarded to the Council and the Commission.

(III) STEP 7: COMMISSION OPINION ON EP AMENDMENTS

(A) IMPACT ON COUNCIL VOTING RULES

The Commission must deliver an Opinion on the EP's amendments. This Opinion is usually the reflection of the comments made orally by the relevant Commissioner in plenary, prior to the vote.

The Commission's Opinion on the EP's amendments is very important as it determines the type of vote necessary at Council level:

- If the Commission has given a <u>negative</u> opinion on at least one amendment, the Council will have to act <u>unanimously</u> as regards acceptance of the EP's overall position.
- If the Commission has given a <u>positive</u> opinion on all the EP amendments, <u>qualified majority</u> is sufficient for the Council if it accepts the EP's text.

(B) TRIALOGUES

Normally, where an agreement at second reading appear to be attainable, informal contacts are established between the co-legislators in order to reconcile their positions. It is necessary because the EP and Council are looking at (and proposing changes to) the same text at the same time, so if they do not informally exchange views, total chaos would arise.

There is no set format for these meetings but, as a general rule, they involve the Rapporteur (accompanied where necessary by shadow Rapporteurs from other Political Groups), the Chairperson of the relevant Council working group (and often the next Presidency representative) assisted by the General Secretariat of the Council and representatives of the European Commission (usually the expert in charge of the dossier and their direct superior assisted by the Commission's Secretariat-General and Legal Service).

The objective is to get agreement on a package of amendments acceptable to the Council and the EP. The Commission's endorsement is particularly important in view of the fact that, if it opposes an amendment which the EP wants to adopt, the Council will have to act unanimously to accept that amendment. This is why any claims by the Commission that they are just 'facilitators' in the process are to be taken with a grain of salt, as they can put the Council and EP under quite some pressure.

If these contacts prove fruitful, the Coreper chair will send a letter to the Chair of the lead Parliamentary Committee, whereby the Council undertakes to approve the EP's amendments if they are in line with the compromise identified jointly. The compromise amendments are then tabled either in Parliamentary Committee or, more frequently, just before the plenary session. They are co-signed for their Political Groups by the Rapporteur and the principal Shadow Rapporteurs, thereby guaranteeing the required absolute majority. The Political Groups within the EP coordinate their votes in order to adopt the amendments negotiated with the Council. If those amendments are adopted in accordance with the agreement reached, the Council will adopt the act and the procedure will be concluded.

(IV) STEP 8: COUNCIL SECOND READING

The Council also has three months (with a possible one-month extension) to approve the Parliaments' second reading text. The time limit starts from the official receipt of the amendments resulting from the European Parliament's second reading, in all the official languages.

The Council's internal procedure is broadly similar to the preparation of the Common Position: the competent working group prepares a position, which is then submitted to Coreper and adopted by the Council.

Two broad scenarios can be identified:

- If the Council, votes by (1) a qualified majority on Parliament's amendments, and (2) unanimously on amendments which have obtained the Commission's negative opinion, and approves all EP amendments no later than three months after receiving them, the act is adopted; and,
- In all other cases, a process known as Conciliation must be initiated.

THE GOLDEN RULES IN SECOND READING

1. If you have done your work correctly in first reading, your focus in second reading should be about preserving what you obtained in first reading. Political deal making is a Brussels specialty and all your efforts in first reading could be destroyed due to an unexpected horse trading exercise. Stay extremely vigilant and make sure that all those that supported you in first reading are reminded of this fact during the second one.

2. Once things go into conciliation, they move pretty much out of lobbyists' scope of action, as discussions are then handled very quickly and compromises struck in all directions, to avoid failure. Even if your objective is to 'kill' a piece of legislation, beware that no legislative measure disappears permanently: it is bound to be resurrected at a later stage.

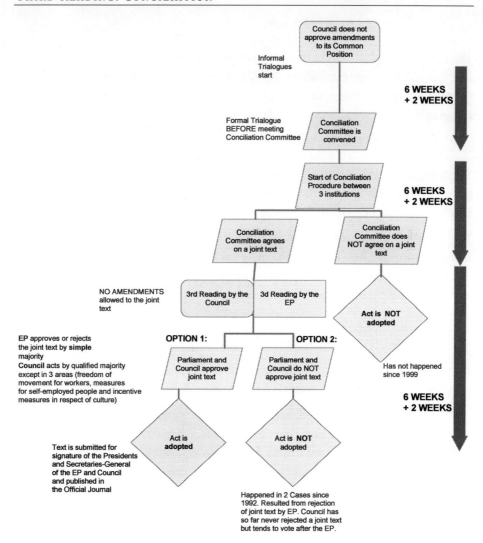

Council does not approve amendments to its Common Position

Informal Trialogues start

6 WEEKS + 2 WEEKS

Formal Trialogue BEFORE meeting Conciliation Committee

Conciliation Committee is convened

Start of Conciliation Procedure between 3 institutions

6 WEEKS + 2 WEEKS

Conciliation Committee agrees on a joint text

Conciliation Committee does NOT agree on a joint text

NO AMENDMENTS allowed to the joint text

3rd Reading by the Council

3d Reading by the EP

Act is NOT adopted

OPTION 1:

OPTION 2:

EP approves or rejects the joint text by **simple** majority
Council acts by qualified majority except in 3 areas (freedom of movement for workers, measures for self-employed people and incentive measures in respect of culture)

Parliament and Council approve joint text

Parliament and Council do NOT approve joint text

Has not happened since 1999

6 WEEKS + 2 WEEKS

Text is submitted for signature of the Presidents and Secretaries-General of the EP and Council and published in the Official Journal

Act is adopted

Act is NOT adopted

Happened in 2 Cases since 1992. Resulted from rejection of joint text by EP. Council has so far never rejected a joint text but tends to vote after the EP.

FIGURE 12-CO-DECISION STEPS 3RD READING (CONCILIATION)

115

(I) Step 9: Conciliation

(A) Composition

The Conciliation Committee brings together members of the Council (usually the Member States' representatives within Coreper) and an equal number of representatives of the European Parliament[47], as well as the Commissioner responsible.

(B) Time limits

The Committee must be convened within six weeks (with a possible two-week extension). It then has another six weeks (with a possible 2-week extension) to reach an agreement.

The objective is to agree on a joint text, with each institution delegation having its own approval rules: qualified majority for the Council's delegation (unanimity in cases where the Treaty specifies an exception to the qualified majority rule) and simple majority for the EP's delegation.

(C) Informal Trialogue:

In practice, a large part of the negotiations are conducted during informal trialogues involving small teams of negotiators for each institution, with the Commission playing a mediating role.

This is mainly due to the fact that the time limits for conciliation are often too short to allow for full-blown official negotiations, especially when the issues at stake are extremely complex and involve a large number of interested parties. As a result, informal contacts frequently occur even before the formal conclusion of the Council's second reading, when it becomes clear that conciliation is likely to take place.

---

[47] In practice, 27 MEPs and 27 substitutes, representing the weight of the Political Groups and usually members of the lead Parliamentary Committee, three EP Vice-Presidents being permanent members of the Conciliation Committee. The EP has put a very detailed and useful Guide about conciliation at http://www.europarl.europa.eu/code/information/guide_en.pdf

In practice, all negotiators involved discuss a four-column document which reflects:

1. The Council's common position;
2. The EP's amendments at second reading;
3. The Council's position on EP amendments (mostly in the form of compromise suggestions); and
4. The EP delegation's position on the Council's proposals.

Any compromise suggestions made by the Commission tend to take the form of footnotes.

This four-column document is extremely complex to read[48] even for seasoned lobbyists and it is not rare for mistakes to occur when putting it together. It is therefore important to at least check if the amendment you follow as lobbyists are properly transcribed in the appropriate columns.

(D) Possible scenarios

There are two potential scenarios for the outcome of a joint text:

- If the Committee cannot approve a joint text by the deadline, the procedure stops and the act is not adopted. It must be said however that this happens rarely and that EU initiatives never truly die: the European Commission will just re-draft them and try again a couple of months (or even years) later; or,
- If the Committee agrees on a joint text, the Council and Parliament have six weeks (with a possible two-week extension) to approve it. The Council acts by a qualified majority and Parliament by an absolute majority of the votes cast. If they do not meet the deadline to approve the text, the procedure stops and the act is not adopted.

(II) Final Step: Adoption or Rejection in Third Reading

The EP and the Council must adopt the act within six to eight weeks, in line with the joint text. Their voting rules differ as the EP only needs a simple majority (majority of votes cast with no possibility to table amendments), and the Council requires a qualified majority (with certain exceptions where unanimity is needed). In the past, there have been a couple of cases where the required majority could not be reached in the EP.

---

[48] See Annex 7 for an example of layout.

3.   CONSENT PROCEDURE

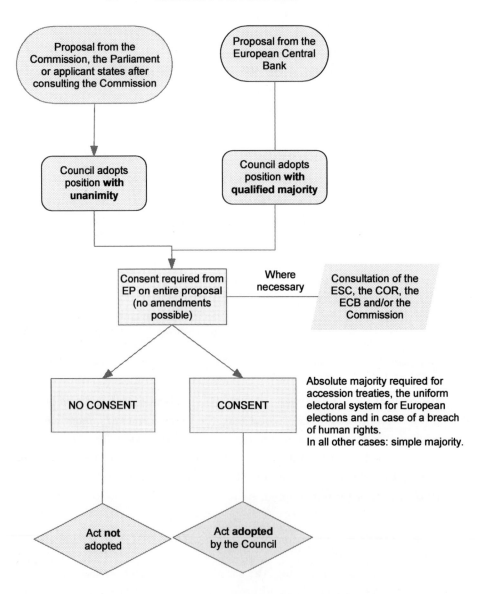

FIGURE 13-CONSENT PROCEDURE

The consent procedure is a form of all-or-nothing co-decision procedure as it requires the approval of the Council and the EP, but the latter can only vote on the entire proposal, in a single reading, and without suggesting any amendments.

Documents required to undergo consent procedure are marked with the code AVC.

Note that legislative measures following the consent procedure are rarely the target of heavy lobbying by industry. This section is therefore mainly for the sake of completeness in terms of all existing EU procedures.

SCOPE / AREAS OF APPLICATION

Originally, this all-or-nothing approach was justified by the fact that consent procedures mainly applied to the approval of international treaties and agreements.

However, the consent procedure's scope of application has gradually been extended to cover the following areas:

- Certain international agreements;
- The accession of Member States and the uniform procedure for European elections - the two subjects where the Parliament must act with an absolute majority;
- Association agreements and other fundamental agreements with third countries;
- Issues relating to citizenship;
- Amendments to the Structural and Cohesion Funds
- Recourse to enhanced cooperation;
- Sanctions imposed on a Member State in the event of a serious and persistent breach of fundamental rights;
- Specific tasks to be entrusted to the European Central Bank; and,
- Amendments to the Statutes of the European System of Central Banks and the European Central Bank (which requires an initial Council position adopted by qualified majority, all the other cases listed requiring unanimity).

4. COOPERATION PROCEDURE

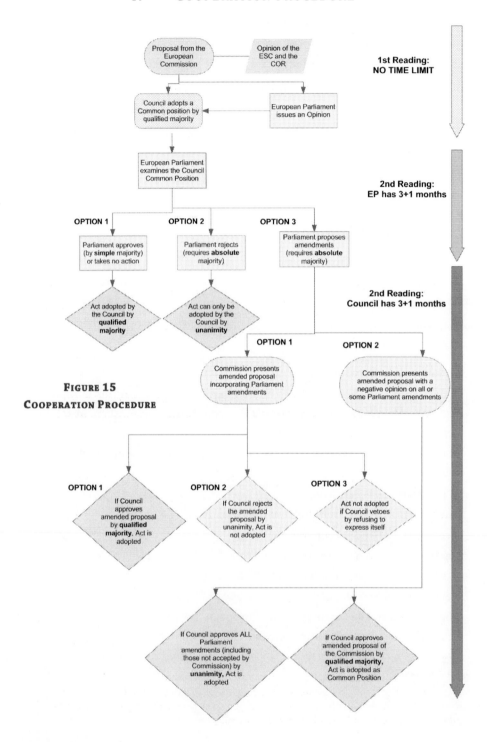

FIGURE 15
COOPERATION PROCEDURE

The cooperation procedure resembles the co-decision procedure in terms of the required dialogue between the institutions and the possibility of two readings, but crucially differs insofar as the Council has the final decision-making power.

Documents that must undergo the cooperation procedure are marked with the code SYN.

Note that legislative measures following the cooperation procedure are rarely the target of heavy lobbying by industry. This section is therefore mainly for the sake of completeness in terms of all existing EU procedures.

DIFFERENT STEPS

At first reading, the EP issues an Opinion and the Council then adopts a Common Position by a qualified majority.

At second reading, the EP has three months to adopt, amend or reject the Council's Common Position, the adoption requiring a simple majority while the amendment and rejection require an absolute majority[49].

The EP's second reading position is examined by the Council, which can either accept it by qualified majority or reject it by unanimity.

In the latter case, the Commission must re-examine the proposal and put an amended version before the Council, which in turn has three months to either:

(1) Adopt the re-examined proposal by qualified majority;

(2) Amend it unanimously;

(3) Unanimously adopt the EP amendments which the Commission has not taken onboard; or,

(4) Exercise a veto by refusing to express itself on the amendments proposed by the EP, or on the amended proposal by the Commission.

---

[49] Rejections by the EP have so far been exceptional and when they occurred, the legislative measure was not adopted, either because the Council could not reach the required unanimity to do so or because the Commission withdrew the proposal.

The cooperation procedure has been replaced in many areas by co-decision, and currently only applies to four areas of the European Economic and Monetary Union:

- The rules for the multilateral surveillance procedure;
- The prohibition on privileged access to financial institutions;
- The prohibition on assuming liability for Member States' commitments;
- Measures to harmonise the circulation of coins.

5. CONSULTATION PROCEDURE

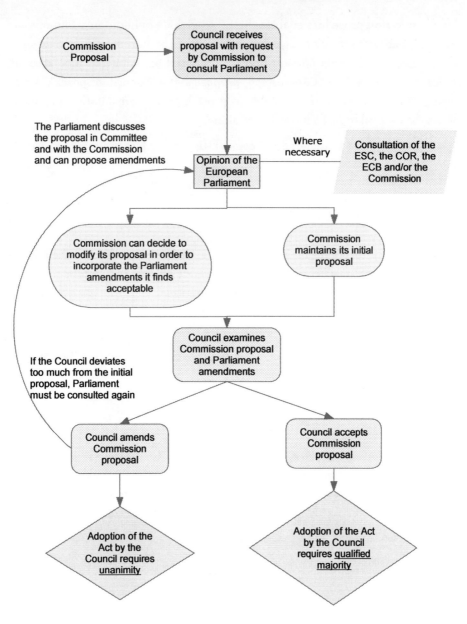

FIGURE 16-CONSULTATION PROCEDURE

The consultation procedure enables the EP to give its opinion on a Commission proposal, but without any obligation on behalf of the European Commission or the Council to take this opinion and its proposed amendments into account. Hence the saying "The Commission proposes, the Council disposes", which implies that contrary to the co-decision procedure, the consultation procedure allows the Council to make its decisions alone.

Documents destined to undergo the consultation procedure are marked with the code CNS.

SCOPE / AREAS OF APPLICATION

The consultation procedure is used in quite a number of areas described in the Treaties, but it can also be used in other areas not covered by the cooperation or co-decision procedures; for example when the Commission considers an issue is important or in case of adoption of a non-mandatory instrument, such as recommendations and opinions.

Obligatory areas set in the Treaties include agriculture, competition, tax, and the revision of the Treaties.

SURVIVAL TIP

The consultation procedure is often relevant to lobbyists that follow recommendations and opinions and want to either use the EP to put pressure on the European Commission or ensure that a recommendation or opinion is either delayed or passed smoothly (as the EP can react more or less quickly in giving its views).

E.   IMPLEMENTATION OF EU LAW

1.   COMITOLOGY

GENERAL DESCRIPTION

Comitology (or Committee Procedure) is a procedure that allows the European Commission to be assisted by a so-called Comitology Committee when using its implementing powers. Comitology Committees are set up by a legal act which authorises their creation, sets under which procedure they will function (see page 125 for the different types of procedures) and defines the content and extent of the Commission's implementing powers.

Comitology is extremely complex and some lobbyists, such as Daniel Guéguen, claim it represents a hijacking of EU power by the European Commission to the detriment of the Council and the EP[50].

COMPOSITION

Comitology Committees comprise a representative of the European Commission who acts as a chair, as well as government representatives of each Member State. Though only advisory, they can also exert some influence: in cases where the Comitology Committee disagrees with the Commission on a draft implementing measure, the latter can be submitted to the Council for a final decision. Such referrals have occurred 17 times in 2004, in the areas of environment, health and consumer protection, and taxation and customs union.

DIFFERENT TYPES OF COMITOLOGY PROCEDURE

Note that due to changes introduced by the Lisbon Treaty[51], it is unclear how comitology will function in the future, as different procedures will apply to so-called delegated acts (which will have a quasi-legislative value, a new aspect introduced by Lisbon) and implementing acts (which correspond to the comitology acts adopted under the pre-Lisbon system).

---

[50] See his book on the matter, « The Comitology Reform », D. Guéguen and V. Marissen, Europolitics, September 2007.
[51] New Articles 290 and 291 TFEU.

(i) Consultation or advisory procedure

Under this procedure, Comitology Committees provide the Commission with their opinion on uncontroversial political issues. Note that the Commission can disregard these opinions.

(ii) Management procedure

This procedure is used mostly for measures relating to the management of the common agricultural and fisheries policies, and the main Community programmes.

If the Commission does not follow the Committee's opinion under this procedure, the Council must be consulted and can adopt a different decision by qualified majority, within a timeframe defined in the initial Decision that set up the specific Comitology procedure.

(iii) Regulatory procedure

The regulatory procedure allows the adoption of two types of measures related to an existing piece of legislation:

- Measures of general scope designed to apply essential provisions of basic legislative measures; or,
- Measures designed to adapt, delete or amend certain non-essential provisions of that piece of legislation.

If the Commission does not follow the Committee's opinion under this procedure, the Council must be consulted and the Parliament must be informed. The Council has three months to approve or adopt a different decision by qualified majority or do nothing (which forces the Commission to present an amended proposal or re-submit the same proposal).

(iii bis) Regulatory procedure 'with scrutiny'

The regulatory procedure 'with scrutiny' was introduced in 2006 and is similar to the regulatory procedure except that it actually gives the Council and EP the right to examine the draft measure and block it if they consider it to either be inappropriate or to extend beyond the powers of the Comitology Committee.

With the Lisbon Treaty and the extension of the EP's powers, this regulatory procedure with scrutiny has become the rule, implying that the EP will have to consent to most decisions reached in the Commission's Committees.

SCOPE/AREAS OF APPLICATION

Comitology Committees exist in almost every sector, with the Commission website listing a total of 295 active Committees in September 2009.

Their meetings are convened by the European Commission and take place several times a year, usually in Brussels. Some of the documents circulated within these Committees are accessible through a search form available on the Commission's web pages dealing with Comitology[52].

ROLE OF OTHER INSTITUTIONS

The EP plays a role in the Comitology procedure as it has a general "right of scrutiny" for draft implementing measures flowing from a legislative act adopted under the co-decision procedure.

In other words, the Commission cannot adopt such an implementation measure without informing the EP and giving them one month to object to the measure.

This right is actually formalised under the 2006 Regulatory Procedure With Scrutiny, which allows the EP (acting by absolute majority) or the Council (acting by qualified majority) to oppose an implementing measure proposed by the Commission under Comitology.

2. AGENCIES

GENERAL DESCRIPTION

Agencies are created by a legislative measure and are usually set up to respond to a variety of needs:

---

[52] See http://ec.europa.eu/transparency/regcomitology/index_en.htm

- The desire by some Member States to introduce geographical dispersal and decentralisation of the EU's activities;
- The need to develop legal, scientific or technical knowhow in certain fields;
- The need to integrate different interest groups and thus facilitate dialogue at European and international levels.

Some would also add that certain Commissioners like creating Agencies to make their portfolio look important. After all, if the EU decides to create an Agency that handles one of your issues, surely you must be dealing with important matters!

TYPES OF AGENCIES

EU agencies all have their own legal personality and are set up by an act of secondary legislation, grouping them into four different categories:

- Community agencies;
- Common Foreign and Security Policy agencies;
- Police and Judicial Cooperation in Criminal matters agencies; and
- Executive agencies.

COMMON CHARACTERISTICS

Although agencies differ in terms of size and purpose, they share a common basic structure and similar ways of operating: they function under the authority of an administrative or management board and are headed by an executive director, nominated by the board or by the Council of Ministers.

Most agencies are financed by a subsidy set aside in the general EU budget for this very purpose[53].

---

[53] However, five agencies are partially or entirely self-financed and can charge fees: the European Agency for the Evaluation of Medicinal Products; the Office for Harmonisation in the Internal Market; the Community Plant Variety Office; the European Aviation Safety Agency, and the Translation Centre for the Bodies of the EU.

F.   NATIONAL LAW–INFRINGEMENT PROCEEDINGS

1.   GENERAL DESCRIPTION

When EU legislation is not directly applicable at national levels (for example in the case of a Directive), each Member State must implement that legislation before the specified deadline and in accordance with certain measures.

National implementation is monitored by the Commission.

If a Member State fails to implement them on time or does so in an incorrect manner, the Commission can take whatever action it deems appropriate in response to a complaint or indications of infringement.

2.   DIFFERENT STEPS

In case the Commission decides to launch a non-compliance procedure against a Member State, the first phase is the pre-litigation administrative phase, also known as 'Infringement proceedings'.

The purpose of this pre-litigation stage is to enable the Member State to conform voluntarily to the Treaty requirements.

There are several formal stages in the infringement proceedings:

- The letter of formal notice represents the first stage in the pre-litigation procedure. At this stage, the Commission asks a Member State to give its comments within a given time frame on what the Commission considers to be an implementation issue.
- The reasoned opinion is a detailed statement defining the Commission's position on the infringement, requesting the Member State to comply within a given time limit.
- The referral by the Commission to the Court of Justice opens the litigation procedure.

SURVIVAL TIP

It is interesting to note that anyone may lodge a complaint with the Commission against a Member State for any measure (law, regulation or administrative action) or practice attributable to a Member State which they consider incompatible with a provision or a principle of Community law, without having to demonstrate a formal interest in bringing proceedings.

In some cases, it is necessary for a company to ask the Commission to initiate such a proceeding, or simply to bring an infringement to their attention. The majority of lobbying in this area is however at the level of moral pressure and threat, as a full blown infringement proceeding rarely delivers its fruits in due time (from a company's perspective).

CHAP. 4: ABOUT WHAT?
THE MAIN EU LEGAL TOOLS

I.   INTRODUCTION

When you lobby European institutions - be it defensively or proactively - it is crucial to understand the legal and moral value of each of the legal measures used by the various institutions:

- To assess the exact impact they may have on you;
- To evaluate the need to lobby them; and,
- To assess how easy it will be to amend them: often, the less binding the instrument is from a legal viewpoint, the easier it is to obtain changes, if you put forward the right arguments.

This section mainly looks at secondary legislation, which is useful for mainstream lobbying. The treaties constitute primary legislation. A short overview is available in Annex 1, as primary legislation is not a usual lobbying target (at least not by industry lobbyists or activists).

II.   THE DIFFERENT TYPES OF EU LEGISLATIVE TOOLS

In terms of secondary European legislation, two main categories can be identified:

- Hard law proposals, which are binding on Member States and for which the right of initiative normally lies with the European Commission; and,
- Soft law proposals, which are non-binding and can be issued by any of the three institutions.

A. HARD LAW PROPOSALS

1. DIRECTIVES

Directives are legal instruments addressed to the Member States, that can be adopted either by the Council in conjunction with the European Parliament, or by the European Commission alone.

Directives require Member States to achieve a certain policy result without going into the details of the methods chosen to achieve it.

Directives usually provide for a timetable for their implementation by Member States into national law (a process known as 'transposition'). Failure to do so by the deadline or improper transposition can lead to the Commission starting an infringement proceeding[54].

Note that following European jurisprudence, Directives can under certain conditions have a direct effect, whereby an EU citizen can ask them to be enforced before a national court of law regardless of their transposition. This means that a lobbyist is less worried about the transposition of such provisions, as Member States must implement them as such (and companies can claim their direct application by Court).

2. DECISIONS

Decisions are legal measures used to give a ruling on a particular issue.

They can be adopted by:

- The Council;
- The Council with the EP; or,
- The European Commission.

Decisions are individual measures (as opposed to regulations), which are binding in their entirety and usually either require a Member State or a person (natural and legal) to take or refrain from taking a particular action, or confer rights or impose obligations on a Member State or person.

---

[54] See page 122 for more details on these proceedings.

A well-known type of Decisions is the one issued by the Competition Commissioner in case of proposed mergers with an EU dimension. Such a decision directly affects the companies involved in the merger, as they can be requested to commit to a certain number of changes for the merger to be acceptable to the Commission. These types of Decisions are clearly lobbying targets, even though competition law dossiers are amongst the most difficult to lobby.

SURVIVAL TIP

Lobbying DG Competition is difficult in general, but becomes extremely risky once they launch an inquiry or handle a merger notification, especially if you are one of the parties concerned. The initiative should be left to them to contact you and ask for your views (or your clients'). Trying to influence other DGs or Commissioners is a pointless exercise, as DG Competition is almighty when it comes to cases pertaining to antitrust law. In some cases, the best route is to use a well-introduced competition law firm, which is likely to have long term established relations with DG Competition in general, and could be able to give you a sense of the 'general mood' surrounding your case.

3. REGULATIONS

Regulations are legal measures which apply in a general manner and can be adopted by the Council together with the EP, or by the European Commission alone.

In other words, unlike Decisions (aimed at specified recipients) and Directives (aimed at Member States), Regulations apply to everyone directly, i.e. with immediate effect and without the need to be transposed at national level first.

A well-publicised example of Regulation is the Roaming Regulation (I and II) which has been adopted at exceptional speed by the institutions and sets the tariffs that must apply within Europe for mobile roaming charges.

Legal measures are built in two parts: the Recitals (first part that starts with 'Whereas') and the Articles (second part that starts with 'Has adopted'). When trying to obtain positive changes in a legislative measure, lobbyists always propose amendments to both Articles and Recitals. As the procedures goes on, it can happen that only the Recital survives the endless negotiations, a result which is much less satisfying than an actual change in an Article, but still worth fighting for. That fight only ceases when the legislation in question is transposed in all the Member States that matter to your client, as Recitals adopted in Brussels are often ignored by the national legislator, especially if they concern the review of an existing Directive (in that case, the revised Recitals are not even included in the final publication in the Official Journal). It is useful to prepare notes linking the Articles to the Recitals that matter to you, and to share this with the civil servants in charge of the process as early as possible.

B.   SOFT LAW PROPOSALS

1.   COMMUNICATION

Most Communications from the European Commission are legislative proposals that end up being adopted as Directives. Green Papers and White Papers (see page 89) are two examples of Communications.

However, in some cases, Communications are also used to indicate that in a specific area, the Commission does not foresee legislative revisions or fundamental change of scope.

2.   RECOMMENDATION

Recommendations are non-binding instruments issued by the European Commission to define its views and suggest a line of action on a specific issue. Contrary to Opinions, Recommendations normally specify the addressee (generally all Member States or in some cases an individual state).

Though Recommendations have technically no legal force, they do carry political weight and can, when linked to provisions in a legal binding instrument (e.g. a Directive or Regulation), even have an indirect obligatory power.

For example, in the telecommunications sector, one of the most heavily lobbied documents is the 'Relevant Markets Recommendation'. In this Recommendation, the European Commission sets out which telecommunications markets should be examined by national regulators in order to evaluate if regulatory obligations must be imposed on certain companies, if they are dominant. Although it is 'only a Recommendation', the related Directives state that regulators have to look at all of these markets, and cannot add any additional markets to the list without the prior approval of the European Commission. For lobbyists, this means that, even if the Recommendation is a 'soft law' tool, it pretty much sets the rules for the telecommunications market in a binding manner and should be a lobbying target regardless of its label.

3. OPINIONS

Opinions are issued by EU institutions to assess a specific situation, development, or individual Member States. In some cases, they prepare the way for subsequent, legally binding acts, or are a prerequisite for the initiation of proceedings before the Court of Justice.

As with a Recommendation, the value of an Opinion is political and moral.

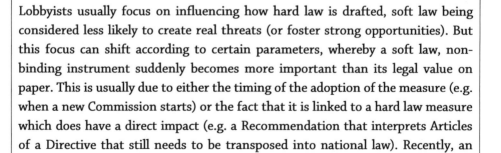

DON'T JUST LOOK AT WHAT IT SAYS ON THE TIN

Lobbyists usually focus on influencing how hard law is drafted, soft law being considered less likely to create real threats (or foster strong opportunities). But this focus can shift according to certain parameters, whereby a soft law, non-binding instrument suddenly becomes more important than its legal value on paper. This is usually due to either the timing of the adoption of the measure (e.g. when a new Commission starts) or the fact that it is linked to a hard law measure which does have a direct impact (e.g. a Recommendation that interprets Articles of a Directive that still needs to be transposed into national law). Recently, an example of such 'relative' weight of EU measures was demonstrated by the intense debates surrounding the drafting of the Digital Agenda, a high-level document aimed to define the newly appointed Barroso II Commission's main objectives and directions for the digital economy portfolio.

Prior to the Commission's proposal of Digital Agenda, a Spanish MEP launched her own-initiative report to determine the EP's wish list, while the Spanish Presidency of the Council proposed its so-called Granada Strategy, a long document hit by so much criticism that it got quickly demoted to the status of Granada Declaration (and lost 40 pages of text in the process).

All of these documents would normally not have hit the radar screen of most lobbyists (as they usually end up being so high level anyone can read and interpret what they want) except for two elements:

1. The freshly appointed Commissioner in charge of the Digital Agenda, Neelie Kroes, said she would take "utmost account" of both. In all fairness, the expression 'utmost account' does not mean much in Brussels-speak but because she was new at handling this portfolio and had been given a rough time by the EP during her selection hearings, no lobbyist would take the risk of interpreting she was merely being polite to later discover she actually did incorporate what the EP and Council put before her. Better safe than sorry, was the general approach; and,

2. There was a rumour of 'Spanish conspiracy' master-minded by a big Spanish telecoms operator (after all, a Spanish Presidency of the Council and a Spanish Rapporteur in the EP, what else does one need in Brussels to start feeling paranoia?).

The result : the wheels of lobbying worked overtime all across Brussels, each document ending up being very neutral due to the opposing interest of all stakeholders involved in getting their amendment included.

PART 2:
EU 2.0 - LOBBYING AND POLITICS IN THE SOCIAL MEDIA AGE

"Social media is like teen sex.

Everybody wants to do it. Nobody knows how.

When it's finally done there is surprise it's not better."

Avinash Kaushik, Analytics Evangelist, Google

I. INTRODUCTION

Web 2.0 and social media are among this decade's biggest buzzwords in the communications world, whether you're talking about marketing, public relations or political campaigns.

As any buzzwords, they can mean a lot of things to a lot of people and so the first step, when talking about Web 2.0, is to simply define what is meant by it.

In this chapter, I will refer to Web 2.0[55] as the online use of social media tools that integrate technology, social interaction and the construction of words, pictures, videos and audio, in order to enable communities to share information, knowledge and opinions. To me, the "2" in Web 2.0 is symbolic of the fact that it refers to a dialogue, rather than a monologue and, guess what: it takes two to start a conversation.

Web 2.0 is basically a web of 'user-generated content' (UGC) and online conversations using platforms like MySpace, Facebook, Twitter and LinkedIn[56].

So from a technical point of view, Web 2.0 is an evolution rather than a revolution of the web. But from a socio-political viewpoint, it represents a fundamental shift in the way politicians interact with society, and in the way society (and lobbyists) can influence politicians.

---

[55] As pointed out by Lon Safko and David Brake in The Social Media Bible, "Web 2.0 is somewhat of a misnomer. It does not refer to a new and improved version of the World Wide Web (...) it's not as though the highway has been widened (...) But (...) there are a lot more interesting vehicles travelling on the highway (...) thanks to Web 2.0 technologies".
[56] A glossary of social media terms can be found in Annex 8.

Books[57], news articles[58], presentations[59] and even more modest blogs[60] link the push for politicians to have a strong online presence, to the 'Barack Obama phenomenon' during the 2008 US Presidential election.

The Obama campaign team and the President himself excelled at using social networking tools to connect and communicate with millions of people.

Just a few figures to prove that point:

- President Obama's campaign team was able to rally five million active supporters across 15 social networks.
- Obama's famous "Yes, We Can speech" was viewed 14,2 million times on his official YouTube page and more than one million times across non-official pages.
- His campaign team posted some 1,800 clips of film footage of Obama while he was running for presidency, generating over a billion minutes of viewership.
- Three million online donors contributed a total amount of US $6,5 million to the 2008 Obama campaign.
- Two million profiles were created on MyBarackObama.com (also referred to as 'myBO'), Obama's own social network, and US $30 million were raised by 70,000 of those profiles through their own myBO fundraising pages.
- The Obama team also used Google Ads to attract donations and potential volunteers.

---

[57] See notably R. Harfoush, Yes We Did ! An inside look at how social media built the Obama brand, New Riders Press ; D. Bullock et all, Barack Obama's Social Media Lessons For Businesses, White Bullock Group ; and K. Kaye, Campaign '08 : A Turning Point For Digital Media, CreateSpace.
[58] See for example an analysis by C. Cain Miller in the New York Times from November 2008 : « How Obama's Internet Campaign Changed Politics »,
http://bits.blogs.nytimes.com/2008/11/07/how-obamas-internet-campaign-changed-politics/?pagemode=print
[59] You can find many presentations on the Slideshare website covering the use of social media by Obama. I like the one entitled : « How Obama Won Using Digital and Social Media »
http://www.slideshare.net/james.burnes/how-obama-won-using-digital-and-social-media-presentation
[60] Just google « Obama social media » and you will find thousands. I enjoyed reading « Web 2.0 Case Study : Barack Obama's Use of Social Media » http://globalhumancapital.org/?p=216

However, it is worth noting that the Obama campaign team used social media to supplement and not to replace more traditional communications methods. This is illustrated by the fact that Obama spent more than double the budget of his campaign rival John McCain on television advertising: between 1 January 2007 and 29 October 2008, Obama forked out US $293 million, compared to McCain's almost meagre-looking US $132 million.

As pointed out by Colin Delany in his e-book *Learning from Obama: Lessons for Online Communications in 2009 and Beyond*[61], "for Obama, online communications was communications, not technology."

In practice, this meant that Obama's online communications team was present at every step of his campaign process and not buried somewhere in the basement with other geeks from the IT department. Also, Obama did not try to reinvent the wheel but combined a few new tools with existing ones, adapting the latter to the specific needs of an electoral campaign (and readapting them yet again after his election to build support for his main dossiers, such as the healthcare reform).

Obama's killer combination was:

- A website (www.barackobama.com), which pushed its visitors towards myBO and was used for messaging purposes;
- An emailing system reaching out to an opt-in[62] database of 13 million names;
- The myBO network and toolkit (with 'walk lists' to visit houses to rally support through door-to-door campaigning, virtual phone-bank applications, fundraising tools, etc.);
- SMS/text messaging; and,
- A strong presence across 15 different social networks, as well as YouTube, Google Ads, and blogs.

In light of Obama's online strategy, the fundamental question for politicians to ask is: Should this remain a campaigning toolkit, or can it be used outside election time, as a way to keep in touch with Joe and Jane Doe?

---

[61] This book can be downloaded at www.epolitics.com
[62] Obama's team was very cautious in ensuring that the people they had in this database had all given their consent to be included and to receive email . Many politicians handle mailing lists less cautiously and can end up irritating the people they send emails or SMS messages to.

I think it can and Obama's team is using the same tools even now to gather support on critical matters such as the health care reform, as well as keep in touch on more trivial matters such as, for example, allowing Internet users to wish the President a Happy Birthday. But few politicians seem to understand how to use it in that manner.

To prove my point, check out the statistics published in the book Politicking Online - The transformation of Election *Campaign Communications*[63]: one year after the German national elections were held in May 2006, only 93 of the 201 candidates' blogs were still active, while 65 had stopped any activity since elections ended and 43 had simply disappeared.

---

[63] Politicking Online – The transformation of Election Campaign Communications, edited by C. Panagopoulos, Rutger University Press, 2009, pg. 188.

II. WEB 2.0: FROM MONOLOGUE TO DIALOGUE

A. RELEASE THE PRESS RELEASE

The toolkit normally used by politicians is a one-way stream of communications, an endless monologue that looks for the electorate's reactive approval.

With Web 2.0, that era of bland statements is gone. Provocatively, self-proclaimed social media guru Brian Solis, summarised this change in his Social Media Manifesto on *The Future of Communications*[64], with the statement "Engage or Die".

Things needn't be that sinister but there is a fundamental truth lurking behind Solis' motto: in a society where citizen journalism is on the rise and people feel that their opinions increasingly matter (as demonstrated by the rise of blogs, vlogs, tweets, Facebook updates, etc), communicating over the Internet must be about interaction.

Essentially, it's about being open to a dialogue with everyone and anyone. It's about accepting constructive criticism and nutty mavericks polluting your space (as is the case in real life, when you think about it). In short, accept to lose control but with a zest of paranoia.

B. PARANOIA IS GOOD; CONTROL IS UTOPIA

Frequently directed at young internet users, the slogan "Think before you post!" should be the guiding principle for any politicians or lobbyist active in the Web 2.0 ecosystem.

Consider it to be the Internet's version of the American Miranda Warning, whereby "anything you say can and will be used against you".

Among the more recent incidents exemplifying how too much spontaneity can backfire relates to the first Twitter[65] steps of EP President Jerzy Buzek aka @jerzybuzek.

---

[64] See http://www.docstoc.com/docs/21771/The-Social-Media-Manifesto-by-Brian-Solis
[65] Twitter is a microblogging site that allows you to send short messages (140 characters) called tweets using your PC or mobile phone. See page 153 for more details.

In the heat of debates surrounding the EP vote on Swift[66], a tweet came from Jerzy Buzek's account stating "I received a call from Secretary of State Clinton on SWIFT indeed", in response to a Twitter query by a journalist. Buzek's tweet was then promptly deleted and its existence denied, even though many users posted screenshots of the original or its re-tweeted version (I was among the latter group and can therefore testify that the controversial Tweet was for real). I believe not much harm was done by issuing this tweet but deleting it clearly revealed an utter lack of understanding of how Web 2.0 works. This is especially true considering that the exchange took place with an accredited EU journalist[67]! Even more importantly, the incident reinforced the fact that anyone interacting on the web must think before they post, or else be ready to face a Twittergate. Once a statement is sent on the web, it is bound to get disseminated, quoted out of context, printed or frozen for eternity through PC 'screenshots. As I summarised it in one of my presentations about EU 2.0: "Paranoia is good. Control is utopia"[68].

You could argue that many of the @jerzybuzek tweets probably came from aides rather than the man himself. Still, they pop up under his name and represent his public e-persona. To think otherwise is frankly naïve. You can avoid trouble though by disclosing upfront that someone else is tweeting on your behalf. No one is amazed to hear that Barack Obama or Jerzy Buzek are not running around thumbing away on their smartphone. The most transparent option is to mention who actually manages your account. On the Twitter page of @barackobama, the background section mentions that the account is run by "Organizing for America", but this is not revealed in the profile statement itself, which is the only thing many Twitter users will see if they use Twitter over their mobile phone or through a separate application[69]. A much better practice example used to be the Twitter account of Nick Clegg, the leader of the UK Liberal Democrats and current Deputy Prime Minister of the UK. His Twitter profile @nick_clegg used to clearly state in his profile that the account is handled by David Angell. This mention was however removed once he became UK's Deputy Prime Minister.

---

[66] Swift in an EU context refers to the EU interim agreement on banking data transfers to the USA via the SWIFT network. This interim agreement created quite some tensions between the Council and the Commission on the one hand, and the EP on the other.

[67] The journalist in question is Daniel Basteiro, and he posted a blog on the incident at www.basteiro.com/313/el-twitter-de-buzek

[68] Presentation on « EU 2.0 : lobbying and politics in the social media age », http://www.slideshare.net/lobbyplanet/140conf-eu-20-lobbying-and-politics-in-the-social-media-age

[69] Separate applications (also called 'Twitter clients') are small softwares one can use to access one's Twitter account without going on the Twitter website page.

FACTS & STATS

The only way to grasp the social media and Web 2.0 phenomenon is to ponder some of the statistics regarding our Internet usage:

- <u>YouTube</u>: Every minute, 13 hours of video footage are uploaded; it would take at least 412 years to watch every YouTube video online; and, every day, more than 100 million videos are watched on YouTube.

- <u>Wikipedia</u>: Over 13 million articles are available on Wikipedia, 3 million of which are in English.

- <u>Flickr</u>: More than 3.6 billion photos are stored on Flickr today, compared to 3.5 million in 2005.

- <u>Twitter</u>: Between February 2008 and February 2009, the number of Twitter users grew by 1,382 percent[70] and about 3 million tweets circulate on Twitter every day. In April 2009, statistics surprisingly showed that the biggest rising demographic on Twitter were the 45-54 years old!

- <u>Facebook</u>[71]: FB is with over 500 million active users (100 million of whom access it via a mobile device) the fastest growing demographic being the 35 years old and older. The average user has 130 friends. More than six billion minutes are spent by Internet users every day on Facebook, while one billion pieces of information are shared each week on that same network, ranging from post and updates, to sharing of links, videos and more.

- <u>LinkedIn</u>[72]: LinkedIn has 75 million members from over 200 countries, with half the members being outside the US.

---

[70] Source: Nielsen NetView, 2/09.
[71] These numbers are constantly evolving. The latest figures can be found at
http://www.facebook.com/press/info.php?statistics .
[72] See for the latest statistics http://press.linkedin.com/ .

III.   The Netpolitics toolkit

This section simply aims to single out some of the mainstream 'must-use' platforms for any politician or institution wishing to interact with everyday people. The list does not pretend to be exhaustive or impartial, nor does it take into account a lot of the very effective tools that have a less global outreach but are very well known and used in certain countries, such as the Dutch social network Hyves or professional networks like Viadeo and Xing, popular in France, Germany and Scandinavian countries.[73]

We will also look at challenges created by the main social media platforms, as well as at basic user guidelines. In addition, the EU Landscape section focuses on the use of social media tools by EU politicians, institutions and officials, and outlines some best practices extracted from actual case studies.

A.   Weblogs/Blogs

1.   Setting up your blog

Blogs are an effective communication tool but only if they follow three key rules: (1) they share stories and not a stream of press releases (2) they are updated on a regular basis, and (3) they accept comments and interact with those that leave a comment.

Figure 18 - Online sources of information used by journalists – Source: George Washington University and Cision "2009 Social Media & Online Usage Study".

In a December 2009 study by the George Washington University and Cision, journalists confirmed that blogs are still one of their main sources of

---

[73] A list of some of the most popular social networks can be found on Wikipedia at http://en.wikipedia.org/wiki/List_of_social_networking_websites

information, just after 'corporate websites'. Blogging should therefore not be handled lightly: as a general rule, it is better not to blog than to do it as an afterthought. Moreover, setting up a blog requires some geeky skills or at least a bit of outside help to ensure that you put together an easy-to-use platform from the back-office side and that it comprises all the expected elements of a blog (RSS feed[74], blogroll[75], possibility to comment, etc.). Personally, I am a big fan of Wordpress but other platforms like Blogger are also user-friendly.

In terms of tone and style, UK Labour politician Tom Harris posted his *Top Ten Tips for Political Bloggers* on his own blog in February 2010[76]:

1. Politics is dull so write at least in an interesting manner;

2. Use humour and don't take yourself too seriously;

3. Go off-topic as the key is to connect with your reader at all possible levels;

4. Don't hesitate to criticise yourself and your party but don't do just that;

5. Allow commenters to have their say, but moderate the loonies;

6. Update regularly;

7. Think about format and design;

8. Be generous on your blogroll, referring both to allies and opponents;

9. If a post is only worth 25 words, write 25 words; and,

10. Synchronise with other platforms such as Twitter, Facebook, etc.

2. RELATIONSHIPS IN THE BLOGOSPHERE

Even if you decide that blogging is not your thing, it is still important to work with bloggers, as they can be a valuable tool in promoting your ideas and profile on the Net.

Blogrolls are useful in that respect, as most bloggers will be warned that you have created a link to their website and are bound to (1) check it out (2) appreciate the gesture and (3) if you are a blogger, to include your blog in their own blogroll as a mutual courtesy.

---

[74] An RSS feed is a web format that allows readers to subscribe to information on the web. Each time you publish new content, your subscribers will be informed of it by email or through a 'feed reader'.

[75] A list of other blogs that you recommend by providing links to them, usually in a sidebar list.

[76] See http://www.tomharris.org.uk/2010/02/10/top-ten-tips-for-political-bloggers/

Moreover, regardless of whether you run a blog or static website[77], make sure that you feature an RSS feed so that bloggers and journalists are easily informed of any updates.

Also, if possible, react (or have your staff react) to posts by other bloggers by leaving a comment on their website or by sharing the link to their post through other social platforms like Facebook or Twitter.

Finally, if you want to raise awareness on certain issues at EU level, the 'Euroblogger' community can be an ally. Sometimes it can pay off to contact bloggers directly to pitch your story to them. So-called Eurobloggers have in some cases filled the reporting gap left by departing Brussels correspondents[78]. They often have solid knowledge of EU politics and like being in the spotlight for their expertise. Moreover, their blogs reach out to readers that are very unlikely to ever read official press releases.

Obviously, putting yourself at their mercy is a risky exercise as they pride themselves of being independent (and in some cases one would say blunt), so you should not do it in a casual or uninformed manner. Read former posts by the blogger in question to ensure that your pitch will be of interest to him or her. Be very transparent about what or who you're representing and what your motivations are for getting in touch. And don't forget: bloggers often quote emails from third parties verbatim in blog posts so be careful how you phrase things.

B. FACEBOOK

1. THE MOST USED SOCIAL MEDIA PLATFORM BY EU POLITICIANS

Facebook (FB) is the most widely adopted social media platform by MEPs: nearly half of them own a profile page, and about one quarter a fan page[79].

---

[77] By static website, I mean a website that is not often updated in terms of its content.
[78] The online EU specialised paper Euractiv.com reported in March 2010 in « Brussels press corp 'shrinking', journalists say », that the number of accredited journalists to the EU had decreased from 1,300 in 2005 to about 800 in 2010. See
http://www.euractiv.com/en/pa/brussels-based-eu-media-shrinking-journalists-say-news-358212
[79] Facebook's competitor MySpace holds a lot less appeal to MEPs, which can be explained by the fact that the site was originally a platform for artists and maybe MEPs feel that whatever they do, "art" is not the best way to qualify it.

Now, at first I wasn't a fan of fan pages because I am naturally wary of being tagged with specific political affiliations – especially in my professional capacity as a lobbyist. However, the 'fan' concept ought to be taken with a grain of salt in the Web 2.0 sphere: it simply does not carry that much emotional weight. Recent changes made by FB itself have considerably improved the terminology: by not talking about being a fan but simply allowing users to click on an "I like" button, the excessive connotation has been removed, making it more likely for politicians to gather more followers.

Moreover, the technical implications of a page Vs a profile justify in the long run why a politician or institution would rather have you as a 'fan'/'liker' than as a 'friend'.

2. COMPARING THE ADVANTAGES OF A PROFILE PAGE VS A FAN PAGE VS A GROUP[80]

Facebook allows users to do three non-exclusive things: create a profile (e.g. John Smith), create a Group (e.g. Wine Bar on Place du Luxembourg) or launch a fan page (e.g. Fans of the EP).

The main limitation with profile pages compared to the other two options is the fact that FB caps the number of friends you can have on a normal profile page at 5000 – obviously a hurdle to some really popular politicians.

WHAT IS A FAN PAGE ON FACEBOOK?

As you can read on the its actual website, "Facebook created Pages when we noticed that people were trying to connect with brands and famous artists in ways that didn't quite work on Facebook…Not only can you connect with your favourite artists and businesses, but now you also can show your friends what you care about and recommend by adding Pages to your personal profile."

So, when you become a fan/liker of a politician or an institution, that information is posted on your 'FB wall'. Your friends can see it too, depending on both their privacy settings and yours. Note that you should be able to check which Pages your friends are fans of via the "Info" tab on their profile.

FB fan pages are quite similar to normal profiles on the site: fan pages have the ability to add friends, and post pictures and videos. In return, fans can leave

---

[80] A third option has become available in April 2010: Community pages, which are intended to be dedicated to a topic or experience that is owned collectively by the community connected to it. These could perhaps be of use to gather a community around a policy debate, e.g. climate change or freedom of speech but are still at early stages of development.

messages on the Fan Page wall[81] and even directly message the people behind the account. Pages communicate by so-called updates, which pop up on the update tab and a person's News Feeds if it's set to display updates. And Fan Pages can have applications as well.

As an illustration, we have inserted below a partial screenshot of Jerzy Buzek's Page on FB:

FIGURE 19 - PARTIAL SCREENSHOT OF BUZEK'S FB PAGE

---

[81] Pages have two walls: One with the posts of the Page owner and with what the fans' messages.

FB Groups can be compared to clubs or associations in the real, offline world: they can be open to the public and welcome everyone, or destined for exclusive members. Their creation takes a bit longer than Fan Pages and requires more information, but at the end of the day, they represent very handy and targeted networking tools.

As an Administrator, you have complete control over your group: you can approve new applicants, invite others to join and appoint Officers who are nominally in charge, but do not have the full administration powers.

You can decide from the start if the group is only accessible to certain networks or to all Facebook users. The Join Permissions setting lets you control if groups are open to anyone, closed (users must get the administrator's approval to join) or secret (by invitation only).

Administrators can invite members to join via Facebook mail and email, and public groups can be found via Facebook search.

SO WHAT TO CHOOSE?

A number of factors can help you determine whether you should opt for a Facebook Fan Page or Group, depending on your activities and goal:

Size matters: As mentioned earlier, the main weakness of a normal profile page is the fact that it only accepts 5000 friends at this stage (rumour has it the number could increase but it's still just a rumour at present). You are also limited in the amount of friends you are allowed to email in one go, as we outline in the 'Email Vs updates' paragraph below. Groups are also directly connected to the people who administer them, whilst Fan Pages, on the other hand, don't list the names of administrators.

Get found: If you are using Facebook for outreach purposes, you obviously want your online presence to be listed in the results of the main search engines. Note that Fan Pages are indexed by external search engines such as Google, just like a public profile, while Groups are not.

Email Vs Updates: As long as a Group has less than 5,000 members, administrators can send messages straight to the Facebook inboxes of each group member. Administrators of Fan Pages can keep their 'groupies' in the loop via updates, which will appear in a specially designed Update section in fans' inboxes.

There is no limit on how many fans you may send an update to, or how many members a Fan Page can have.

<u>User control:</u> Because of their 'private club' character, Groups offer far more control over who gets to participate. Access to Fan Pages, however, can only be restricted by certain ages and locations (e.g. Fans have to be from Belgium and over 18 years old).

<u>Applications:</u> Fan Pages can host applications, which give them a personalised touch and allow them to display more content, while Groups can't.

<u>The bottom line:</u> Groups are great for organising human interaction on a more personal level and smaller scale. Fan pages are better for brands, businesses, music bands, movies, or celebrities who seek to interact with their fans or customers on larger, perhaps more anonymous scale. Note that you can create events and advertisements on both Fan Pages and Groups.

For politicians and institutions, I'd recommend using Fan Pages, especially since potential followers now do not have to say they are a 'fan' but simply 'like' your page.

Though not analysed here as it is an external application from Facebook itself, it is also worth noting that you can use an application called Causes[82] on Facebook (and on MySpace), that can be useful when running a campaign on a specific subject.

---

[82] See http://exchange.causes.com/about/

To summarise:

Profile	Fan Page	Group
Cap of 5000 friends	No cap	No cap
Linked to a person	Not linked to a person	Linked to its Administrator
Person communicates with Friends	Page communicates with Fans	Administrator/creator communicates with Members
Communication by email capped to avoid spam.	Communication appears in "Updates" section of each fan's news feed.	Burst emails capped to groups of less than 5000 members appear in Inbox.
Actions by Friends, such as wall comments, will appear in their News Feed (viewable by their friends) unless they have set privacy options preventing this.	Actions by Fans, such as commenting on the wall, will appear in their News Feed (viewable by their friends) unless their privacy settings prevent this.	Actions by group members appear in their Highlights/Event feed **only** if the group is set as Global and Open – Closed or Secret groups do not appear in non-members' news feeds.
	Pages may only be restricted by certain ages or locations	Groups, as mentioned above, can have restricted access and membership.
Pages can be customized with applications.	Pages can be customized with applications.	Groups cannot use applications
Anyone can create a profile.	Pages can only be created to represent a real public figure, artist, brand or organization, and may only be created by an official representative of that entity	Groups can be created by any user and about any topic, as a space for users to share their opinions and interest in that subject.
Listed in search results of search engines like Google.	Listed in search results of search engines like Google.	Not listed in search results of search engines like Google.

C.   MICRO-BLOGGING: TWITTER

1.   TWITTER, TWEETS, HASHTAGS, BIRDS AND WHALES

Twitter is a free social networking and micro-blogging service that enables its users (aka twitterers) to send and read messages of up to 140 characters known as tweets. These tweets are displayed on the author's profile page and delivered to the author's subscribers, known as Followers. Twitterers can restrict their page to friends by locking their account or, by default, allow open access.

Twitter has some particularities worth noting before you start using it:

- <u>Birds and whales:</u> Twitter's logo is a cute little birdie, which has become a very recognisable symbol for the platform. Buttons and Twitter widgets can be integrated in websites, Facebook and so-forth, showing either a "t" or a bird to encourage users to follow you on twitter. Moreover, when the network reaches over-capacity, users see a Fail Whale error message, which shows an illustration of red birds using nets to hoist a whale from the ocean.

FIGURE 20 – SOME EXAMPLES OF THE MANY ICONS USED TO LINK BACK TO TWITTER ACCOUNTS

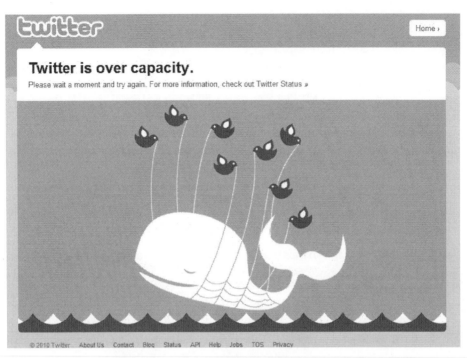

FIGURE 21 - THE FAMOUS 'FAIL WHALE' IMAGE

- <u>Hashtags:</u> It has become an ingrained convention among Twitterers to distinguish content by using semantic tags (aka keywords), preceded by the hashtag symbol #. This enables other users to search and filter tweets based on those key terms. It also allows sharing relevant information, and enables 'trending' (as displayed on the Twitter.com homepage) or 'live-tweeting' (see the specific paragraph below). European-related news for instance is usually marked by #EU. But you can also add other hashtags, referring for example to the context (e.g. #swift during the SWIFT debate); the institution (European Parliament officials tend to use #ep); or Presidency communications (e.g. #eu2010 used by the Spanish Presidency of the EU). There are also Twitter-specific hashtags, like #ff or #followfriday which is used by Twitterers every Friday to draw attention to those Twitterers they like best and encourage others to follow them too. There's also the very (in)famous #fail, used to qualify anything considered as a failure or dysfunction. As you can imagine, this can come in quite handy when tweeting about EU affairs.

- <u>Re-tweets (RT):</u> When you like a tweet, you can 're-tweet' it (in a similar fashion to 'forwarding' an email), either without comments or with some additional text (expression such as 'LOL' for 'laughing out loud' or '+1' to show you agree with a tweet are quite common).

- <u>Live tweeting</u>: When attending events, Twitterers will tweet about what is said by presenters, note reactions in the room or even their own, post pictures of slides or the location, re-tweet tweets from other people following the same event, etc. This is a great way to create a 'buzz' around an event and should be organised beforehand by any politician, institution or lobbyist setting up an event. It is also a good way to gather new followers that might discover you because they are interested in that event and appreciate the fact that you are live tweeting it.

- <u>Links</u>: Sharing information and links is key when using Twitter. Due to the short nature of the tweets, links are inserted through so-called URL shorteners, frequently embedded now into Twitter tools themselves.

- <u>Timeline (TL)</u>: Your twitter time line refers to your tweets and/or the tweets of those you follow on Twitter, displayed in real time order.

2. 140 CHARACTERS: JUST WHAT YOU NEED...OR NOT?

THE PRO'S: SHORT IS GOOD

Even though only about a third of MEPs and three European Commissioners currently have an account, Twitter is actually a very approachable social media platform. It certainly requires a lot less effort than writing blog posts or even maintaining a certain level of activity (beyond status updates) on Facebook or other similar social networks. 140 characters are often just enough to share a link about something you find interesting, post a picture on Twitpic (or another platform), or share personal views. And the best bit is that a tweet is short enough to avoid putting your foot in your mouth (unless you're Jerzy Buzek, of course).

I'd recommend to any politician (aspiring or established) that they register their name on Twitter, even if they don't plan to use it religiously. This avoids others using your name on Twitter, often for satirical purposes. This is for example the case with the German Commissioner Günther Oettinger: the twitter account @goettinger which is a fake account issuing very funny tweets. If you're faced with the dilemma of a long name – remember that the 140-character rule does not just apply to tweets but also to your 'twitter name', which is included in case of re-tweet - pick a shorter version which remains identifiable to your target public. For example the German MEP Reinhard Bütikofer uses his nickname @bueti as his twitter handle.

Moreover, once you are active on Twitter, it is considered offensive, not to mention useless, to simply wait for Followers without following anyone. You should at the very least follow fellow colleagues or industry peers, as well as official information sources of the EU institutions. The very basis of Twitter is about exchanging ideas, not just broadcasting your own messages. It's a dialogue, remember.

Interestingly, the UK government has put together a *Template Twitter Strategy for Government Departments, which* describes "why and how [they] intend to establish and manage a corporate presence" on Twitter. Definitely a must-read for any EU player[83].

THE CON'S: LACK OF CONTROL

Twitter presents some major pitfalls regarding the amount of control you exert over tweets:

- What is posted in the Twittersphere lives on forever: sure you can delete a tweet but don't be fooled into thinking that you've cancelled out its existence. It is still out there, somewhere, in a cached version of your page, in a re-tweet before you hit delete, in a screenshot taken by a careful surfer. In contrast, it's usually a lot easier to permanently delete a status update on Facebook.

- You have no control over what people say to, or about you on Twitter: you can delete comments on Facebook, but on Twitter, you can only erase your own tweets, not those of fellow Twitterers.

- Whatever you tweet will be re-tweeted or quoted out of context: imagine a follower has tweeted some provocative stuff at you and you eventually reply with a snotty remark. Guess what? Chances are your nasty comeback will hit the headlines, and not the tweets that lead to it.

- Whatever you do, don't block journalists or other public figures from following you on Twitter: there are online tools which will reveal your action, and the shunned are likely to report it as an unwillingness to be scrutinised and reported on.

---

[83] See
http://blogs.cabinetoffice.gov.uk/digitalengagement/file.axd?file=2009%2f7%2f20090724twit ter.pdf

- The Twitter community is currently still quite specific. A fellow Twitterer came up with the following distinction between Twitter and Facebook: "Facebook is a more advanced tool for simple people while Twitter is a simple tool for more advanced people". In other words, most people on Twitter are not just there to read a status update and glance at your latest YouTube post, but to engage with you, often in a constructive manner.

These challenges are obviously the same for politicians or lobbyists, and the damage a single inappropriate tweet can cause can to a certain extent explain why most could still feel uncomfortable with this medium.

In the UK, a Labour MP candidate was sacked from the party for tweeting that he disliked organic bananas and wanted "a slave-grown, chemically enhanced, genetically modified one"[84].

In the US, Sarah Palin is famous for her tweets. Her tweet that people should *'refudiate'* plans for a New York City mosque near Ground Zero and the fact that, when criticised for using an non-existing word, she compared herself to Shakespeare launched a flurry of comments on Twitter and in mainstream media[85].

D.   FORMAL PLATFORM: LINKEDIN

1.   MORE   CONTACT   DATABASE   THAN INTERACTIVE PLATFORM

A Business Week article called LinkedIn "Facebook in a Suit"[86] back in 2008. But frankly, if the "suit" image is accurate, the level of interaction you get on LinkedIn is minimal compared to Facebook (even though LinkedIn is trying to change this).

Platforms like LinkedIn do not require anywhere near as much maintenance as Facebook or Twitter, since people do not expect you to post updates or regularly update your profile.

---

[84] See http://www.spectator.co.uk/coffeehouse/5900493/labour-candidate-wanted-slave-grown-banana.thtml
[85] See http://www.guardian.co.uk/news/blog/2010/jul/19/sarah-palin-refudiate-new-word or http://voices.washingtonpost.com/44/2010/07/palin-invents-word-compares-he.html
[86] See
http://www.businessweek.com/the_thread/techbeat/archives/2008/10/linkedin_launch.html

Moreover, thanks to the add-ons available on LinkedIn, you can easily integrate other social media tools like your blog and tweets into your LinkedIn profile. In other words, once you have taken the time to fill in your professional profile and resume, you can pretty much leave LinkedIn to its own devices. This is a great business platform for contacting people you have just met or to be contacted. The mood is definitely one of professional networking for job searchers and recruiters, with more than 60 million registered users from over 200 countries.

2.   BUT STILL WORTH 30 MINUTES OF YOUR TIME

For a lobbyist, LinkedIn is a good platform to be spotted on by potential clients, and maintain contact with people they've just met.

For a politician, it can be a low maintenance way to reach out to professional connections. I consider it especially useful if you want to publicise an event or create a Group around a specific issue or campaign.

But if you do put a profile on LinkedIn, make sure that it is kept up-to-date. A bad example of this is Secretary of State Hillary Clinton whose LinkedIn page in June 2010 still listed 'Candidate at Hillary Clinton for President' as her current job title. Maybe she left it up for next US Presidential elections[87]?

FIGURE 22-SCREENSHOT OF HILLARY CLINTON'S LINKEDIN PROFILE

---

[87] See blog post at http://www.localseoguide.com/senator-hillary-clinton-back-in-the-race/

E.   VIDEO: YouTube, Vlogging and going viral

Uploading a small video onto your blog (also known as vlogging) and/ or YouTube can be a very effective and attractive way for conveying a message.

You can either create your own clip or post short movies you've enjoyed watching. Maybe they help underline a message you want to convey in a blog post.

However, producing online videos requires following some basic rules:

- The average YouTube video is less than three minutes long[88], so don't start filming a sequel to *Gone With The Wind* if you do not want to turn off users.

- Make sure to 'tag' your uploaded video with clear, specific keywords so that it can be easily searched for: there are more than 200,000 videos published on YouTube everyday so you need to ensure yours is findable.

- Customise your user background: this takes only a couple of minutes and makes visitors' experience more personal. You can use the same background for both your YouTube and Twitter accounts for example.

Viral videos are typically humorous videos posted by users and which spread over the Internet in a virus-like manner: everyone gets them quickly. In politics, most of the known viral videos relate to US politics. There is of course the famous Obama Girl video posted by an eager fan of the then presidential candidate Barack Obama. The video featured an unknown Amber Lee Ettinger singing "I Got a Crush on Obama". To date, it has been viewed and shared more than 100 million times, and was extensively covered in the media.

The tricky bit happens when politicians or political parties try to launch viral videos on purpose because an adviser or their young geeky nephew told them it was a good way to reach out to a younger audience.

---

[88] The maximum allowed length by YouTube for an uploaded video is 15 minutes.

STOP! THE VIRAL VIDEO ROUTE IS PAVED WITH DANGER:

First of all, creating a viral video as a politician or political party is of no value if it does not in some way reflect your message. Sure a funny video of you clumsily dancing or falling from the stairs could go viral, but it will not tell viewers why you matter as a politician. Being eyeballed by the world without anyone remembering what you stand for is not very effective, unless you consider people remembering your name as your main goal. However, viral videos can also simply be used as an initial hook to gather interest.

Secondly, viral videos created by politicians themselves often miss the mark completely, as Internet users have a natural unwillingness to accept "crafted" viral videos[89]. This is especially true these days for so-called LipDubs, i.e. videos of politicians who lip-sync a famous song. LipDubs featuring the Black Eyed Peas' "I Gotta Feeling" song with an awkwardly dancing politician belong in the sin bin.

Finally, a viral video runs the risk of being spoofed, responded to, mocked and turned against you either by your opponents or by bored Internet users looking for a bit of fun. So be prepared to handle such actions gracefully or steer clear altogether.

F.   PICTURES SPEAK MORE THAN WORDS: FLICKR / PICASA AND TWITPIC/TWEETPHOTO

Posting pictures online is always a nice way to show people what you are doing and what you like. Neither do you need to splurge on special equipment, as a simple mobile phone with a camera can do the trick.

In addition, it can turn a rather dull tweet such as "Visiting the employees of factory Y" into a slightly more personal message if you add a link to a picture of that visit.

Then again, don't go overboard with this. A perfect illustration is the mayor of London, Boris Johnson (aka @MayorofLondon on Twitter), who appears to post

---

[89] There are however exceptions such as the very well-thought series of videos by Hillary Clinton (when running for the Senate), in which she made fun of her singing abilities, asked people to vote for the best song amongst a list and then concluded with a parody of the last episode of "The Sopranos" with her husband Bill.

an image with every second tweet. Most of these photos show the same Boris in different places.

Obviously, putting high-quality pictures of yourself on sharing sites like Flickr or Picasa, is always useful in case journalists or bloggers want to write about you (just make sure you don't infringe the photographer's copyright). But what is even more interesting is to show the public your vision of the world. Dutch MEP Marietje Schaake (aka @MarietjeD66 on Twitter) shares her thoughts and (dis)likes, by posting pictures of the pile of papers she still needs to go through on a given evening, of a beautiful landscape she is looking at, or a live scene of the EP plenary.

Of course as per usual, think before you post. Unlike Vincent Van Quickenborne, the Belgian Minister for ICT, Telecoms, Economy and Reform, who was reprimanded by none other than the Prime Minister for posting pictures of a Council of Ministers meeting[90]. Then again, this mini-Twittergate also made Van Quickenborne quite popular in the Twittersphere.

G. Online Advertising: the example of Google Ads

The use of advertising by politicians is still not a very established practice in Europe, and currently mostly entails the use of banners and similar Web 1.0 tools during election campaigns. The same cannot be said for American politicians, who excel at using advertising not only to draw votes but, more importantly, also to raise funds.

In this section we look at the example of Google Ads, as it is a reasonably cheap way to advertise for a politician. Other platforms such as Facebook also offer advertising possibilities. Basically, a politician can write a short ad, tag it with keywords (e.g. labour, elections, etc.) and when people search for these keywords using Google search, or go to websites comprising these keywords, the ad gets displayed.

---

[90] He also posted pictures of his naked feet under the table during a Parliamentary Committee meeting, showing how the heavy snowfalls had made him remove his wet and frozen socks and shoes. These were equally pointed out as "inappropriate" by some.

An interesting anecdote is worth mentioning here, as it could indicate how Google Ads could be used in the future, if not officially by politicians themselves, by third parties wishing to make a point.

Following a very harsh article about the UK Labour Party in the *The Sun* newspaper, Internet users discovered that anyone typing 'Labour' into the Google search engine the next day was met with a sponsored link pointing to the home page of the party's official website, and a subtitle reading *"You can't trust The Sun. Wrong on Hillsborough, Wrong on Labour"*. The incident was also reported on in the press[91].

FIGURE 23 – SCREENSHOT OF THE GOOGLE ADS (RIGHT COLUMN) REGARDING THE SUN

The UK Labour Party denied that it was responsible for the adverts - which were taken down promptly- and chances are it was indeed the action of Labour supporters or activist groups acting independently. But the incident showed how Google Ads can be a reasonably cheap way to convey a given message in relation to a specific search query by an Internet user. This could certainly become an increasingly relevant manner to interact with internet users regarding specific campaigns and issues.

---

[91] See article on the UK Telegraph site
http://www.telegraph.co.uk/news/newstopics/politics/labour/6247256/Pro-Labour-Google-adverts-attack-Sun-over-Hillsborough-disaster.html

H.   Regardless of the Tools: Registering your name and Integrating are Key

Everyone has to decide for themselves what their preferred social media toolkit mix is.

But two principles should **always** be considered:

1. Register your company, Political Group or personal name on as many platforms as possible to avoid domain squatters[92]or simply homonymous users; and,

2. Use tools[93] that integrate as many platforms as possible and can be used both on your computer and your smart phone. This will allow you to synchronise your status updates across all platforms automatically if you wish to do so. It also lets you consolidate your various platforms into one single application, which helps streamline your social media interaction. Also, use each platform to boost others: tweet the link of your latest blog post or your latest Facebook note, embed your latest YouTube in a Facebook update and a blog post, etc.

IV. EU Web 2.0 landscape: a traditional approach with some remarkable exceptions

An increasing number of studies look at how EU institutions in general and MEPs in particular use Web services and tools[94]

It is actually disappointing to note that, whereas the EP, both as an institution and through its individual elected officials, tries to reach out online (be it timidly), the European Commission seems to make no real progress. Commissioners are rarely present on the Internet in an interactive mode and the official channels use these new tools in a rather limited manner.

---

[92] People that register your name to either (1) stop you from using it, (2) use it to make fun of you or (3) try to sell it back to you.

[93] These are often free softwares such as Tweetdeck, Twittelator or Hootsuite.

[94] See notably Fleishman Hillard (2009). *European Parliament Digital Trends*. See: http://www.epdigitaltrends.eu/

It must be said, however, that not all institutions have been created equal and the structure and spirit of each EU institution very much determines its external (non-) communication strategies. Regardless of the good will of people inside these institutions, there are fundamental differences between the European Commission and the EP, which shape the way in which they behave and spread the e-word.

The Council has been discarded in the following analysis because it is the least transparent of the three EU institutions and therefore very unlikely to show truly innovative usage of social media in the short or mid-term (though one can always remain hopeful to see a behavioural shift some day).

A.   EUROPEAN COMMISSION

1.   ONLINE PRESENCE

The European Commission obviously has its own website, in addition to all those of the various Commissioners and Directorate-Generals. There are also dedicated websites for specific projects (e.g. the site dedicated to '2010 European Year for Combating Poverty and Social Exclusion'[95]). All of these sites tend to form a maze that is a definite handicap in terms of identity creation and message streamlining.

There are also a series of blogs by individual Commissioners, which sadly rarely feel very interactive or spontaneous (except for the blog of former Communications Commissioner Margot Wallström, and the posts by current Commissioners Kristalina Georgieva and, quite recently, Commissioner Neelie Kroes): many of them read like slightly modified press releases mixed with travel/ meeting schedules (e.g. "Today I met the delegation X at Y and we talked about Z").

The Commission's use of other Web 2.0 platforms is still very nascent and depends more on the willingness of individual Commission officials to engage in online interaction, than a deliberate strategy by the institution itself.

The paragraphs below show the state of play in June 2010[96].

---

[95] See http://www.2010againstpoverty.eu/?langid=en
[96] A good list of EU institutions on Facebook and Twitter can be found at http://europa.eu/take-part/social-media/index_en.htm . Blogs are listed at http://blogs.ec.europa.eu

(1) COMMISSIONERS

Four current Commissioners have a blog: Kristalina Georgieva, Andris Piebalgs, Neelie Kroes and Maria Damanaki.

Commissioner Georgieva's team have found the right tone and rhythm for their posts. The same is true with Damanaki's blog (although one can regret the lack of pictures), Maria Damanaki having started blogging long before becoming a Commissioner. Piebalgs' blog tends to be a bit more formal and curt.

The most interesting blog to evaluate is however Commissioner Kroes'. Funnily, her blog featured fake filler text, more than one month after being appointed in charge of Europe's Digital Agenda. Needless to say, the EU Twitterati had a field day hashtagging this.

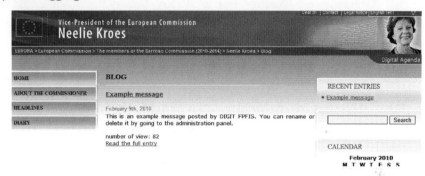

FIGURE 24-SCREENSHOT OF COMMISSIONER KROES' BLOG IN MARCH 2010

But instead of taking this the wrong way, her communication team seem to have taken on the challenge and the blog is now very well done (the same being true in terms of her Twitter and FB presence, as we show in the sections below). The blog posts talk about real life experiences (such as receiving an SMS from her mobile operator with a message that annoys her) and includes a nice mix of videos and professional looking pictures as well as mobile phone pictures.

The only thing still missing on her blog is the ability for readers to comment, a function which is enabled on the three other Commissioners' blogs.

Kroes was interviewed by the Commission's social media team in August 2010 about her use of social media, an article which gives interesting insights in how someone with her responsibilities and hectic schedule handles the web 2.0 dimension[97].

Several elements in her responses are worth noting:

1. The fact that she has the proper tools installed on her mobile phone to use platforms such as FB and Twitter;
2. The fact that even if she admits she is not always in a position to post messages herself directly, Kroes has entered into 'web 2.0' mode in terms of thinking (even when she does not have the time to post herself, she passes the ideas on to her cabinet members;
3. Her interest in entering into a dialogue and the fact that she does not take criticism personally; and,
4. The fact that she considers social media as a way to inform about what she does, which implies she first needs to do the job, before 'tweeting' about it.

Note that Commissioner Reding has a 'Video Gallery'[98], which could be considered a form of 'vlog' (blog through videos), even though the very formal nature of the videos misses web 2.0 spontaneity.

(II) OTHER

A few EU Representations[99] have blogs. The Commission website list Belgium, Estonia, Spain and Finland but it is worth checking any representation relevant to you, as they all have their own websites and some adopt a writing style one could consider as informal as blogging. Their websites can be accessed at http://ec.europa.eu/represent_en.htm .

The Innovation Policy unit of DG Enterprise has also set up a blog[100] in July 2009, initially in the context of a panel discussion on business innovation. The blog was kept however as an ongoing initiative, but it hardly seems a success, with only one blog post per month on average, and a readership of 100 to 150 web-users.

A more interesting initiative is the 'Waltzing Matilda' blog put together by the Commission's Social Media section within the Europa.eu web team. Because it is run by a few civil servants that really try to preach the web 2.0 wonders to their colleagues in the Commission, it assembles all the right ingredients: a variety of writers (senior officials, trainees, external guest bloggers, etc.), stories and

---

[97] See http://blogs.ec.europa.eu/waltzing_matilda/kroes-social-media-means-talking-with-europeans/
[98] See http://ec.europa.eu/commission_2010-2014/reding/multimedia/videos/index_en.htm
[99] Representations are EU 'embassies' in Member States.
[100] See http://blogs.ec.europa.eu/innovationunlimited/

interviews, insider information on how the team works (and sometimes suffers). And readership is actually quite high (500 to 900 views), especially considering the blog was launched in April 2010.

TWITTER

Four Commissioners, namely Janez Potocnik (@Potocnik_Janez), Neelie Kroes (@NeelieKroesEU), Kristalina Georgieva (@k_georgieva) and Maria Damanaki (@damanaki) tweet on a regular basis. Funnily enough, the people responsible for social media in the Commission's communications team were unaware of the two latter Commissioners' Twitter presence until someone – well, me – told them so. Using Twitter.

A number of Commission services use Twitter to post links to press releases and updates on their department's website.

EU representations also have Twitter accounts: UK (@EUlondonrep), Ireland (@Eurireland), the Netherlands (@EUinNL), Spain (@UEmadridrep), and Cataluña (@ComissioEuropea).

Equally present on Twitter are some European Agencies (the European Training Foundation @europa_etf, the Office for Harmonisation in the Internal Market @oamitweets and Eurofound @eurofound) and specific projects and/ or events (e.g. @ict2010eu or @GreenWeek).

Moreover, career and selection procedures are increasingly broadcast via Twitter thanks to an account oddly named @EU_Raconteurs.

And finally, there are individual civil servants acting in a semi- private / semi-professional capacity trying to make Europe more accessible through their tweets[101].

The end result: a flurry of twitter accounts with no clear policy in terms of the chosen twitter names (even 'EU' becomes 'UE' in some cases, if it appears at all), and probably only people inside the EU bubble able to map all of them and make some sense out of it.

I queried with members of the Commission social media team why the Commission as institution did not have one single twitter account (e.g. @europa_ec) and use hashtags to differentiate between policy areas, events, etc. The structure of the institutions was the main hurdle quoted back at me[102].

---

[101] See notably @dicknieuwenhuis , @Anne_EU_Webteam @euonymblog and @TonyLbxl.
[102] See our full analysis below in the Section 'Hurdles', page 168.

Though there are quite a few Facebook profiles and pages of Commissioners, few are legitimate. Word on the street is that the European Commission will put up an official European Commission page, soon-ish.

The one element of communication the Commission seems comfortable about is promoting recruitment and careers within the institution. Two dedicated Facebook pages have been created - EU Careers and EU Careers Raconteurs - to advertise events, answer questions about the selection procedures, post updates about competitions and so on.

Group pages have been created officially by EU Delegations outside of Europe (notably in Morocco and Russia) and EU Representations (Germany).

YOUTUBE:

The European Commission has its own YouTube Channel since 2006, called EUTube[103]. Several Commissioners such as Kroes[104] have their own separate YouTube channel, but with very few viewers.

The Commission also has a European Union TV information service called Europe by Satellite (EbS)[105], which notably broadcasts live coverage of EU press briefings, EP plenary sessions, or European Council meetings, in audio and/or video formats.

2.   HURDLES

As pointed out above, regardless of the strategies and good intentions that can be brought together at an institutional level, the structure and functioning of a given EU body does weigh heavily on its communication possibilities and approach. The Commission has a number of characteristics which could make a fully-fledged adoption of social media difficult, if not impossible.

---

[103] See http:// www.youtube.com/user/eutube
[104] See http://www.youtube.com/user/NeelieKroesEU
[105] See http://ec.europa.eu/avservices/ebs/welcome_en.cfm

Collegiality: the Commission is the sum of its Commissioners (or less)

The Commission works according to the principle of collegiality, meaning that decisions are supposed to be made collectively by the College of Commissioners and not by individual Commissioners.

The fact that the Commission is the sum of its Commissioners is not fundamentally different to national governments but seems to create even more challenges at EU level, maybe due to this "collegiality" principle[106]. But in terms of communications, that sum can actually sometimes result in a negative outcome.

Moreover, the Commission's President often relies heavily on the Secretary-General in terms of keeping the troops coherent and 'on message'.

As a result, most Commissioners simply prefer to stick to the "official line" as it clearly takes a strong personality to dare act spontaneously in terms of messaging. Commissioners' staff members in turn are extremely cautious and prefer to say "no comment" when in doubt in terms of external messaging. All this is obviously rather incompatible with social media which in turn requires speedy actions and spontaneous lightness in tone, not lengthy screenings and standardised press release speak.

Mia Garlick, the Australian Assistant Secretary General for Digital Economy and a member of the Government 2.0 Task Force, brilliantly summarised this antagonism in her blog 'The Faceless Bureaucrat and Web 2.0'[107]:

> "There are some inherent tensions between the practice of Web 2.0 and the practice of Government. Web 2.0 tends to be characterised by a sense of the personal, a sense of immediacy and a sense of informality. All these things mean that mistakes in the Web 2.0 world can and are made readily but are equally readily corrected, sometimes by the original contributor, sometimes by the crowd.
>
> The practice of Government, on the other hand, tends to be the opposite of each of these things. Instead of being personal, we have the stereotype of the "faceless bureaucrat". Instead of being immediate, Government announcements and actions can take a while to be forthcoming while all

---

[106] As a reminder, this principle implies that Commissioners should not act individually but collectively with their 26 colleague Commissioners. See page 30 for a detailed description of the Commission.

[107] See http://gov2.net.au/blog/2009/08/17/the-%E2%80%98faceless-bureaucrat%E2%80%99-and-web-2-0/

possible stakeholders are consulted and points of view are considered. Instead of being informal, Government-speak is quite formal with each word chosen very carefully. Government processes are set up to minimise, if not completely avoid, the chance of making a mistake."

WILLINGNESS TO COMMUNICATE: A NON ELECTED BODY

The European Commission has been facing an identity crisis in the communications field for ages. For most European citizens, Europe and Brussels, as Capital of Europe, are associated with stuffy bureaucracy and technical measures that only become relevant when introduced at national level by their own government. The European Commission has been trying for ages to 'connect' with EU citizens through big online debates, consultations and advertising campaigns. So why is it seemingly failing in its efforts? The answer is simple: because no one at the Commission is elected.

This has two consequences:

- On the one hand, it is difficult to build a link with citizens if they have no say in the appointment of your leadership, or of anyone within your institution, for that matter; and,

- On the other hand, why would the Commission feel pressured into communicating when it is not facing the prospect of elections and accountability to citizens?

Luckily, Commissioners and staff often take pride in their work and do consider it important to communicate EU-related matters, if only to make citizens feel concerned and implicated. But the structure of the beast makes their attempts often anecdotic rather than the rule.

DECENTRALISATION: BUILDING MULTIPLE LAYERS OF COMMUNICATION

The Commission is a decentralised institution:

- At a <u>geographical</u> level: there are officials in charge of communication both in the Brussels headquarters Vs representations and delegations in Member States and third countries; and,

- At a <u>structural</u> level: each Commissioner has a spokesperson, but DGs also have communications teams, as do agencies and representations spread over the world. These different channels do not always get along with each other and have different levels of jargon (the DGs often producing technical documents that then get painfully translated into slightly less jargon-heavy political speeches that rarely go beyond the EU specialised press)[108].

Commissioner Viviane Reding[109] was reported by the press as stating at her first internal meeting with the Communications Directorate that the Commission Representations "are the eyes and ears of the Commission" and must be on the front line of EU relations with the citizens. It is understandable that in some cases, a communications official in a given country is best placed to know how to communicate locally. Explaining an EU issue to a farmer in Romania or a young student in Milan should be approached differently, and the EU ivory tower in Brussels is not always best placed to do so. It's not only a question of language, but also of cultural empathy and awareness of the local interests and challenges.

But despite this well-meant approach, the layered approach to communication in the European Commission creates substantial challenges that explain the fact that no magic formula has been found yet.

CULTURE: TURF & CONTROL

The European Commission's main issue regarding the use of Web 2.0 tools is the fact that they have an ultimate urge to control every single piece of communication leaving the institution. As a result, many of their tweets or Facebook updates end up being links to official press releases or, in bolder initiatives, an official EU video clip.

Moreover, the overlapping portfolios of the different Commissioners mean that everyone is extremely sensitive about claiming their turf and, more importantly, stopping any other service from threading on it. This seems hard to reconcile with social media and the era of spontaneity and dialogue.

---

[108] As shown in our overview of the EU 2.0 landscape, this decentralisation is also reflected in the fact that each Commissioner, DG, representation, etc. have their own website (usually within the ec.europa.eu domain).
[109] Who is currently in charge of Communications and the very heavy Justice, Fundamental Rights and Citizenship portfolio. (communications being considered as part of the Citizenship element).

WHEN COMMISSION OFFICIALS SEND AN OPEN LETTER TO THE COMMUNICATIONS COMMISSIONER

The frustration must have been brewing for some time inside the European Commission when its Web editors and Webmasters wrote an open letter[110] to the President of the Commission in January 2010, asking him and the new Commissioners to integrate Web 2.0 into the institution's communications strategy. Among the list of recommendations from the civil servants, the following seem especially relevant in light of this book's analysis:

- Strip European Commission sites and pages of obscure jargon and less relevant content (e.g. historical backgrounds, sites of ex-Commissioners, etc)
- Encourage/ empower Commission staff to use social networks and make them aware that this requires a continuous online presence.

The letter ends with an excellent description of how the European Commission has handled communications so far: "We will need a major shift in attitude to break away from the one-way, top-down communication culture, still prevalent in many parts of the organisation, and develop an in-house communication culture that encourages and empowers staff across the organisation to use the internet to interact with people."

The response[111] however is less than encouraging, with minor recognition of the need to use social media immediately tempered by a need to be careful in terms of resource allocation. According to internal sources, the Commission seems to have decided to move extremely cautiously regarding social media, preferring to focus its resources on improving its existing pool of websites.

The online newspaper Euractiv published[112] a leaked letter from Commissioner Reding to Barroso showing her 'master plan' for Commission communications, which aims at more centralisation and a greater emphasis on President Barroso's personality as leader of the Commission.

---

[110]   See   http://dicknieuwenhuis.files.wordpress.com/2010/01/open-letter-final-january-2010.pdf

[111] See http://dicknieuwenhuis.files.wordpress.com/2010/05/cab03_0510102652_001.pdf

[112] See http://www.euractiv.com/en/future-eu/commission-plans-communication-revolution-news-497233

B.   European Parliament

1.   Online Presence

In terms of the EP's online presence, it is useful to distinguish between the institution itself on the one hand and the MEPs on the other hand.

The institution

The EP website has improved quite considerably over the past years in term of usability, and has the advantage of communicating via a single website, as opposed to the Commission's loosely coordinated network of separate websites. The only EP person to own a separate website from the institutional one is the actual President[113], who gives an interesting overview of his activities (in terms of speeches and agenda), the team surrounding him, and comprises links to his Facebook and Twitter accounts.

The paragraphs below show the state of play in June 2010.

(i) Blogs

The EP as an institution needs to be differentiated from the individual MEPs: the institution's communication goal is after all to 'sell Europe' as a story, while MEPs are trying to 'sell themselves' in order to be re-elected.

Although many MEPs run blogs, these can in no way be seen as representing the views of the institution. The 'official' EP blog is *Writing for (y)EU*[114], put together by the institution's own Web editors will be analysed in more detail below.

(ii) Twitter

The EP has several Twitter accounts, which issue similar messages but in different languages (@Europarl_EN for the English version, @Europarl_FR for French and @Europarl_DE for German), as well as a separate Twitter account for their TV items (@europarltv), which informs of every newly posted film.

Some of the EP's Web editors and spokespeople also have their individual accounts[115], which they use in a semi-private/ semi-professional capacity,

---

[113] See http://www.europarl.europa.eu/president/view/en/the_president/latest_news.html
[114] See http://www.ep-webeditors.eu/

combining Tweets about their latest jogging achievement with information about the institution and/ or their working experience.

(III) FACEBOOK

With over 75,000 fans, the EP's Facebook page[116] is certainly quite successful and not only communicates EP activities on a regular basis but organises live chats with MEPs responsible for hot topics.

(IV) YOUTUBE & OTHERS

The EP has its own YouTube Channel since 2007[117], as well as its own TV channel called EuroparlTV[118]. EP videos are also available on Vimeo[119].

The EP is also present on Flickr[120], My Space[121]and Flavors.me[122].

MEPs: TIMID BUT INCREASING STEPS

If many MEPs have discovered the Internet (or at least their assistants have), most have remained safely tucked away in Web 1.0 and refused to go beyond conventional websites.

According to the EP web editors' blog, usage figures of April 2010 are as follows[123]: 55 percent of MEPs are now on Facebook (i.e. 401 MEPs with a total of 454,000 fans), 38 percent have a blog (282 MEPs), and 31 percent are on Twitter (230 MEPs with a total of over 114,000 followers).

But having a presence on social media platforms does not necessarily mean that you're actually using them (let alone using them properly).

While about one third of MEPs are discovering social media tools and creating profiles and accounts, a majority of these early adopters by EU institutions

---

[115] Notably @tayebot , @stctweets, @jduch, and @mvandenbroeke .
[116] See http://www.facebook.com/europeanparliament
[117] See http://www.youtube.com/EuropeanParliament
[118] See http://www.europarltv.europa.eu/
[119] See http://vimeo.com/user2682029/videos
[120] See http://www.flickr.com/photos/european_parliament
[121] See http://www.myspace.com/europeanparliament
[122] See http://www.flavors.me/European_Parliament
[123] See http://www.ep-webeditors.eu/2010/04/how-may-meps-use-social-media-a-tentative-update/

standards[124] still remain either extremely passive in the use of these tools, or very traditional in their approach (e.g. by merely posting links to their latest press release or, for the daring, their blog post).

It is also striking that the online activities of many MEPs, especially on micro-blogging sites such as Twitter, seem to have started during the pre-electoral phase in early 2009, and then abruptly ended in the first weeks of July that same year, once elections were over.

The fact is that MEPs represent the interests of the national constituency who vote for them. Put differently, MEPs may be symbolic embodiments of European democracy but they are not representatives of the EP as an institution.

European Political Groups in turn have a broader EU dimension but obviously focus their external communication on the messages that correspond to their political affinity and opinions. The main Political Groups typically use most of the web 2.0 tools (dedicated YouTube channels with clips of MEP speeches and other short films, Twitter accounts, Facebook pages, more or less interactive websites, etc.) but many are still a bit traditional insofar as they still tend to opt for a 'broadcast' rather than a true dialogue mode. I once had a funny Twitter exchange with a Political Group, during which I politely suggested that they (1) stop sending 15 Tweets within 10 seconds about some YouTube video they just posted because this was slightly "polluting" my Twitter timeline, and (2) indicate the speaker and topic rather than tweeting a URL with the words "Speaking time political party X at plenary". Their response came two days later telling me that (1) it was an automatic feed and (2) to just click on the link to find out whom the speaker was. Guess what: I un-followed them.

On a more positive note, when I reacted to a another Political Group's spokesperson tweeting that he wanted to use a hashtag with the symbol '&' by pointing out that this was not an accepted character by Twitter in hashtags, the said spokesperson very professionally thanked me and changed the hashtag in question.

2. TYPICAL EP TRAITS: A WILL TO INTERACT

AN ELECTED BODY WITH MEDIA-HUNGRY POLITICIANS

The EP is the only European institution to actually be directly elected by citizens (since 1979), which means that (1) every five years, each individual MEP is made

---

[124] Institutions by nature tend to be much slower than individuals. The EU's pace is specifically slow in terms of accepting and implementing change.

accountable for their actions, and (2) that the institution's public impact is measured by the percentage of people motivated enough to vote. In addition, the EP's ratio of 736 politicians to around 5,000 civil servants makes for smoother external communications compared to the European Commission which boasts 27 politicians for about 25,000 civil servants.

In other words, it's in the EP's interest to reach people on the streets because essentially, if no one hears or cares about the institution, few people will bother to turn up to vote, which in turn undermines the institution's *raison d'être* as a whole[129].

WHEN THE EP DISCOVERS TOO MUCH OF A GOOD THING CAN HURT

The EP has also had its share of clumsy campaigns subject to subsequent mock attacks. The most recent concerns 'Citzalia', an online role playing game currently in development phase and paid for by the EP. The game site states that "Citzalia is democracy in action. It is a role-playing game and social networking forum wrapped in a virtual 3D world that captures the essence of the European parliament"[125]. Users can create their own avatar, explore a virtual parliament and debate on various EU related topics, characters and environment having a 'cartoony' look. The site should be fully functional by the end of 2010 / beginning of 2011.

The project was brought to public attention by a well-known euroblogger, Jon Worth,[126] and soon picked up by the Guardian[127] and various other mainstream newspapers. Criticism ranged from questioning the usefulness of the project and the fact that the budget allocated to it could maybe have been used for other purposes, to a general mood of surprise after one of the consultants responsible for the project complained about Citzalia being 'a victim of the blogosphere' in the press[128], pointing a finger directly at Jon Worth. It is too early to guess if the project will be a success but its launch is certainly not one to be immensely proud of, in terms of social media management skills display.

---

[125] See http://blog.citzalia.eu/about-citzalia/
[126] See http://www.jonworth.eu/citzalia-the-virtual-ghost-european-parliament-really-why-spend-money-on-this/
[127] See http://www.guardian.co.uk/world/2010/aug/06/eu-parliament-role-playing-game-online
[128] See
http://www.royalgazette.com/rg/Article/article.jsp?articleId=7da85ab30030009&sectionId=65 and Jon Worth's response at http://www.jonworth.eu/oh-so-citzalia-is-all-my-fault/
[129] The turnout for the 2009 EP elections was the lowest so far, with only 43 percent of potential voters actually voting (see
http://www.europarl.europa.eu/parliament/archive/elections2009/en/turnout_en.html).

Though the EP's work is split up between various specialised Committees and Delegations, and between Brussels and Strasbourg, the institution itself is a rather monolithic and coherent body. The best indication for this is the fact that the EP's Web editors and press officers have been consolidated into a single department (even if the press officers speak for various specific committees).

This means the issues of turf , 'left hand not knowing what the right hand is doing' syndrome, and the inherent over-cautiousness present in other institutions are a lot less pronounced at the EP, and hence do not inhibit communication (as much).

V.   EU 2.0 KNOW-HOW

Let's be honest: there is no right way of communicating on the Web. There is only one fundamental rule: stay honest, as any lies or inconsistencies will be unveiled at some stage.

There are nevertheless some tips about how to avoid Web pitfalls and instead achieve positive results, as exemplified by successful cases of politicians or institutions in the EU 2.0 arena.

A.   CASE STUDY: THE SUCCESS OF A FRENCH SECRETARY OF STATE

In the study 'Comment les Ministres et Secrétaires d'Etat utilisent-ils Twitter?', the communications company 2803media analysed the (more or less) successful Twitter presence of French government representatives and linked their online activities to four types of messages (see Figure 25):

1.   The governmental related messages: what meeting they are attending, their ministry's latest press release, etc.;
2.   The professional messages related to other mandates they have (e.g. as mayor);
3.   Replies to other Twitterers; and,
4.   Personal information (e.g. last holiday destination; stuck in traffic; fan of a particular artist, etc.).

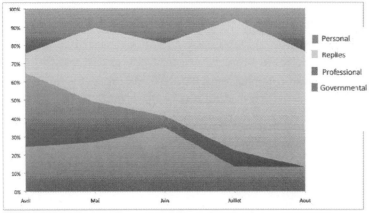

Nathalie Kosciusko-Morizet– source 2803 MEDIA

FIGURE 25 – NATURE OF TWEETS FROM N. KOSCIUSKO-MORIZET – SOURCE: STUDY
'COMMENT LES MINISTRES ET SECRETAIRES D'ETAT UTILISENT-ILS TWITTER?",
2803MEDIA

Politicians should note that a mix of all four types of messages is required to maintain a strong presence in the social media ecosystem. In the French case study, the Minister/Secretary of State with the most followers is Nathalie Kosciusko-Morizet (nicknamed 'NKM'). Since joining Twitter in February 2009, she had gained nearly 8,500 followers by mid-September, having published all but 465 tweets. In June 2010, she had reached over 45,000 followers with just under 1200 tweets. Her online success can be explained in part by her personality and portfolio (as she is in charge of the digital economy) but possibly even more so by her social media know-how.

Kosciusko-Morizet seems to grasp who her target audience is and how to reach them effectively. She moved very quickly from a monologue to a dialogue mode, with more than half of her tweets now replying to Tweets sent by her followers. She also skilfully posts about one fourth of personal messages without actually divulging much of her private or family life.

B.   European case studies: a chatty Dutch MEP and the EP web editors

1.   MEP...and Technically-savvy?

Looking at MEPs' Twitter activities[130], successful MEPs by Twitter standards usually follow the same pattern as Kosciusko-Morizet, even though some MEPs such as Daniel Cohn-Bendit (over 5,400 followers) maintain a high number of followers despite a complete lack in 'Twitter action' (Cohn-Bendit managed a meagre 25 posts and stopped tweeting completely after the June 2009 elections). The most active MEPs on Twitter seem to be the Dutch, such as Jeanine Hennis-Plasschaert[131] (more than 6,500 followers and 10,000 tweets as an MEP), Sophie in't Veld (over 5,900 followers and 5,000 tweets), Wim van de Camp (over 4,500 followers and 2,700 tweets) and Marietje Schaake (nearly 2,900 followers and over 4,200 tweets). On a side note, German MEP Reinhard Bütikofer (over 2,200 followers and 2,500 updates) is also well ranked.

In short, if you're a famous public figure, you don't need to necessarily tweet a lot to gain followers (as demonstrated by the Cohn-Bendit account). But the real benefit of the Twitter platform lies in its capacity to create a true interaction between you and your followers. To me, the most successful MEP in that regard is Hennis-Plasschaert aka @JeanineHennis, who tops the charts of EU Twitterers, according to EuropaTweets. She was kind enough to share some of the key elements of her winning Twitter strategy for the purpose of this book:

- A certain degree of geekiness: I don't want to sound sexist but let's face it, statistics show the average MEP is a 50-year old male. And going beyond statistics, it is still common to enter an MEP's office and find neither a computer on their desk, nor a smartphone in their hand. Tech-savvy MEPs and other EU decision-makers who own a smartphone and personal laptop (maybe even with applications not officially authorised on the hardware supplied by EU institutions...Hush!) definitely stand a better chance to succeed in the online environment.

---

[130] The number of followers and tweets in this paragraph reflect the situation in June 2010 and rely on data collected by http://www.europatweets.eu , a private site that collects and aggregates tweets from EU officials.
[131] The latter left the European Parliament in June 2010 to go back to national politics in the Netherlands.

- **It's a fun past-time, not a burden**: When asked why she was so active on Twitter and Facebook, Hennis-Plasschaert's reply was very simple: "Because it's fun". In her opinion, social media tools allow her to have an immediate contact with people she would not have time to interact with otherwise due to her hectic schedule; to have her viewpoints challenged by followers and to hear their concerns. She also revealed that she tweets to relax in between two meetings or while using public transport. In short, it's not an activity which has to be fitted into her agenda.

- **A democracy-enhancing tool**: For Hennis-Plasschaert, Twitter and other social networking tools can help bridge the gap which exists between everyday citizens and EU institutions, and contribute to more direct democracy (as it allows people to participate directly in political discussions). She revealed that she had tried to convey her enthusiasm for social media to colleagues but, while some seemed to suddenly 'see the light', others seemed to treat it simply a channel to issue press releases or worse, just a burden.

2. THE EP WEB EDITORS: SETTING THE RIGHT TONE

Another good example of successful e-communication is given by the team of Web editors who maintain the EP's official website[132], as well as their own blog[133]. They take the same dual approach to Twitter, where official EP accounts (depending on language) mingle with those of the EP editors who communicate in a much more relaxed manner with fellow Twitterers.

A definite advantage, the EP Web editors have a clearly defined messaging strategy set out in a post entitled *The day We Invented The Synopsis*[134], which reveals how the team managed to tackle their biggest communications hurdle: "How do you write an article in 22 languages about the very same subject without translating it?".

Their use of synopses and the freedom of each individual team member to "tell the story" according to their own culture and inspiration is part of the success of their messaging. In addition, they post an interesting mix of information and some personal stories on their blog, which provides an insider's view into what life is like in an EU institution, or for an expat in Brussels.

---

[132] See http://europarl.europa.eu
[133] See http://www.ep-webeditors.eu/
[134] See http://www.ep-webeditors.eu/2008/07/the-day-we-invented-the-synopsis/

But this approach, as interesting and well-balanced as it may be, is unlikely to come to the attention of the mainstream citizen or even media, as long as there is no direct link featured on the home page of the EP website. Web editors (or should I say 'EP'?), take note.

C.   A WORD OF WARNING: TOO MUCH WEB 2.0 KILLS WEB 2.0

There is obviously a risk with Web 2.0 tools, and that is that you can over-use them (as demonstrated in the Citzalia example).

For instance, I don't believe that imitating President Obama's social media strategy during the electoral campaign would make much sense within a European context. Let's face it: Europeans react differently to political messaging, political parties do not use the same fundraising logic and frankly, regardless of where you live, the general tendency among Internet users these days is to shout: "Please: not another social network!"

French President Nicolas Sarkozy's political party (UMP) learnt this the hard way and in a very mediatised manner, when it launched its own social network called Creators of the Possible: after five weeks, with only 8,000 registered users and a flood of mockery on the Internet and TV, this initiative – presented as a 'revolution' – faltered. A perfect example of how too much Web 2.0 can backfire in a big way.

At EU level, it makes much more sense to use the current social media tools and not add yet another layer to an already crammed online environment (see our comments on Citzalia).

D.   SOME GUIDELINES TO DO THINGS THE RIGHT WAY

As mentioned earlier, the attempt to turn Commissioners into bloggers fails if their contributions read too much like press-targeted content. In all fairness, given a Commissioner's tight schedule, blogging often simply proves too time-consuming. Instead, micro-blogging platforms such as Twitter could offer easy-to-use and highly effective alternatives.

But even if an institution is willing to adopt the tools, the real challenge for successful external communications lies in striking the right balance between:

- Building a **story**;
- Creating a **voice**; and,
- Embodying a **face**.

More precisely:

- The **story** is usually the tip of the iceberg which everyone concentrates on within EU institutions. Successful examples are stories like "The Commission was able to decrease your mobile roaming charges" or "Europe is simplifying paperwork for cross-border divorces".
- The **voice** of an institution is the communication channel providing easily accessible information about its daily activities and why Mr and Mrs Doe should care. It can be a tweet by @eu_eeas, a press briefing by the spokesperson, a press release on Rapid[135] and so on.
- The **face** of the institution is made up of those individuals that help you 'relate' to the institution. They are the ones that make you think you want to engage not out of duty, but as a citizen, a human being, a mom, an angry teenager, etc. Good examples are the blog by the EP Web editors (Writing for (y)EU), the tweets of @dicknieuwenhuis, @euonymblog, @Dana_Council or @jeaninehennis who tell you what they are working on, why they are shocked by a certain press coverage, what Ambassador they talked to, and so on.

Every time I read something about EU Communications, the tagline seems to be: we need to have a **story** to sell and do so with one **voice**. That is in part true but it shouldn't be just about that. The important bit is to create a **face** for Europe, and not just stick to the **story/voice** bit. It is obviously a challenge, but some seem to get it so why not rely on them to help other institution members to make the shift?

---

[135] See http://europa.eu/rapid/

THE GOLDEN RULES TO USING SOCIAL MEDIA

In summary, the key guidelines to using social media tools are:

1. <u>Be there:</u> Register your account on every platform you are likely to use and even on those you are unlikely to use, if only to avoid that someone domain-squats your name. This can be done using a tool like Namechk[136], which allows you to verify whether your username or vanity URL[137] is available at popular social networking and bookmarking websites.

2. <u>Show your human side:</u> Publish a balanced mix of personal information (without going all the way to the cheesy "eating yoghurt with muesli"[138]) and political messages.

3. <u>Act in real time whenever possible:</u> Post your status updates while you're on the move. Hot-off-the-press news is so much more exciting than status updates that refer to a well-thought but often unemotional and delayed press release.

4. <u>Speak, listen, reply:</u> Web 2.0 is about a two-way flow of information: you talk/you listen, you speak/you answer, you share/they react.

5. <u>Paranoia is good – control is utopia:</u> Reacting quickly does not mean you have to throw cautiousness out the window, quite the contrary. Everything you tweet or post can and will be used against you, forever.

6. <u>Link and sync when appropriate:</u> Even though there are aggregators that allow you to post the same update on different platforms, not all updates are appropriate everywhere so think before you synchronise. As regards linking, post links to things you care about and this without having to go on a treasure hunt (it's just so painful when the posted link goes back to a home page rather than the relevant page of the site).

7. <u>Please the eye:</u> Add the occasional visual element, as pictures and videos always offer a nice touch and are usually not likely to be controversial.

8. <u>It won't kill you to be funny</u>...Seriously.

---

[136] See http://namechk.com/

[137] A vanity URL is a URL or domain name, created to point to something to which it is related and indicated in the name of the URL. Social networking sites like Facebook offer vanity URLs so that your page appears as www.facebook.com/nameofpolitician instead of www.facebook.com/randonstringofnumbers

[138] The Belgian Finance Minister Reynders is so famous for tweeting about weather that he is informally referred to as the weatherman by Belgian Twitterers, who like to send him tweets asking for his weather forecasts.

VI. Are EU Lobbyists entering the iLobby Age?

A.   Lobbyists as slow adopters

Lobbyists tend to be a cautious breed and they have been very slow to adopt social media tools. This is true regardless of location, even though lobbyists in the US are probably getting up to speed a lot quicker than their EU counterparts.

The two main reasons for this are: (1) many lobbyists are not digital natives, and (2) many lobbyists like to consider their trade as a mysterious business, requiring secretive one-on-one interactions with decision-makers at boring cocktails and sandwich lunches.

Clearly, the direct human interaction element in lobbying is still predominant and unlikely to ever disappear. And yes, in most cases, discretion is an ally while loud campaigns a sign of defeat. Moreover, a bad tweet or an improper Facebook update (too sinister, too funny, or too something else) can cause real damage. But social media offer many interesting uses that nicely complement traditional lobbying.

B.   Why iLobbying should form part of your strategy

I am yet to be convinced by some lobbying courses' claim that "social media are a key component in European lobbying".

An article comparing the use of social media by American and European lobbyists, found that "it could be some time before the internet replaces cosy chats over a cup of tea as the most effective means of influencing politicians"[139].

Nevertheless, I have found that my use of social media has given me a competitive edge over some of my more traditional colleagues, as set out below.

---

[139] 'Suspicious minds - how lobbyists use social media', Communicate Magazine, February 2010, see http://www.communicatemagazine.co.uk/archive/90-february-2010/1002-suspicious-minds

1. SOCIAL MEDIA AS SOURCE OF INFORMATION

The social media platforms are great tools to stay informed about what's happening in Brussels and beyond, especially when you realise that a lot of journalists, academics and activists use social media in a quite transparent manner. This really helps to put your finger on the pulse of time and public opinions.

Personally, I follow for example Twitter peers on other continents because I know that they will provide me with relevant information on dossiers relating to their part of the world, the same way I post EU information. This gives me an instant and sanitized feed of relevant information from specific people (specialised press, academics, activists, etc.) whose expertise and knowledge I trust.

I also follow live tweets of events to gain a sense of what's happening, in case I do not have time to watch the actual live stream (or if none is provided).

In some cases, I will pick up gossip and be able to put together pieces of information that are not important enough to make it into the headlines but that can still give an insight into a given subject. For example, the tweets between MEPs are a good way to gauge which MEPs are natural allies on a given subject (in some cases regardless of their political affiliation) and which are likely to disagree. Some MEPs also tweet about the lobbyists they meet, allowing me to react (ask for a meeting too, have a chat with their assistant(s), etc.) should I read that a certain MEP is meeting with a stakeholder that has opposite views than one of my clients.

2. SOCIAL MEDIA AS A NEW WAY TO INTERACT

Social media allow you to connect with activists, politicians, civil servants and citizens interested in EU-relevant matters, in a manner and to a scope that is simply impossible to replicate in real life or "IRL" (as geeks qualify interactions that do not involve a computer screen). In real life, you usually target a given set of policy-makers who can be a fairly small group, particularly if you lobby a specialised area. With social media, you are able to easily broaden your scope, seeing that "following" someone on Twitter or "befriending" them on Facebook does not require the same effort or commitment as an actual physical meeting.

Reacting to a status update by approving, sending an information link, or disagreeing in a polite and well-argued way can start interesting discussions with a politician or journalist. Sometimes, a first contact on Twitter or Facebook can lead to a real-life contact in a much more informal manner than an official request per e-mail.

Moreover, in my case, I have found that my Twitter name @linotherhino triggers an instant recognition and a smile among some policy-makers – a reaction my real name would not usually get during a first encounter. In fact, I was once greeted by an MEP in a corridor of the European Parliament as Ms. Lino The Rhino.

3. SOCIAL MEDIA AS A NEW WAY OF CAMPAIGNING

So-called grassroots campaigning can be an effective way to convey a message because it shows that a certain cause matters to people on the street. Social media and the Internet in general can obviously be an excellent way to raise awareness about an issue and enrol people's support in an efficient and non-costly manner.

This is true for both companies and activists wishing to lobby a particular issue, even though activists and NGOs are often more likely to come across as credible in online campaigns (and less timid) than multinational corporations.

The two case studies below offer an illustration of how to use social media to campaign on a policy issues.

In July 2009, eBay launched a campaign asking their users to sign a petition to change EU regulations that let luxury brands put limits on who was allowed to sell their products online.

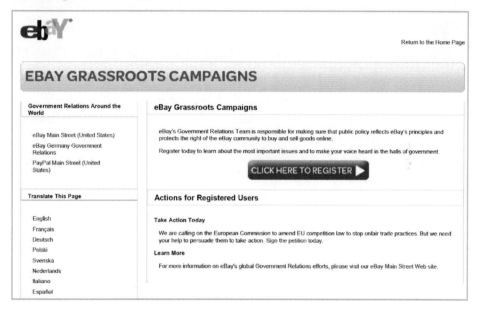

FIGURE 26- SCREENSHOT OF CAMPAIGN BY EBAY

The result: more than 750,000 signatures were collected across Europe, of which over 250,000 came from the UK, 200,000 from Germany and 100, 000 from France. Even more interesting was the acknowledgment by a vast majority of those signatories that they would be interested in joining similar eBay campaigns in the future.

The campaign was spread across multiple levels in the form of (1) a special button on the home page of eBay websites; (2) emails sent to all eBay-registered users with the subject heading: "Fighting for your right to buy and sell online", (3) ads in local newspapers and (4) people collecting signatures on the street.

Unfortunately, the campaign had little visible impact on the policy-making process, and the European Commission refused to meet eBay representatives in front of the press to receive the signatures. This prompted eBay to put up huge billboards displaying the number of signatories at every metro exit near the Schuman roundabout – where thousands of Commission and Council staff commute to for work on a daily basis.

La Quadrature du Net describes itself as "an advocacy group that promotes the rights and freedoms of citizens on the Internet". Based in France, the non-profit activists became very visible at European level when a French debate known as Hadopi or Three Strikes found its way into European discussions taking place in 2008/9[140] regarding the review of the electronic communications legislative package.

La Quadrature was very much in favour of a controversial amendment to the EU Telecoms package[141], and used all its online tools to stir up support by combining:

- A so-called blackout action supported by many Internet activists[142] and which saw users replace their usual avatars[143] with a black square showing grey EU stars and the mention 'Blackout Europe', when the crucial EP vote was getting closer. This action made the movement very visible in places like Facebook and Twitter or when people posted comments on blogs;

FIGURE 27-BLACKOUT EUROPE AVATAR

- A very comprehensive and constantly updated Wiki[144] of the legislative amendments, backgrounds, etc.;

- Co-ment, an online toolkit allowing vetted specialists to collaboratively annotate and write amendments for proposed legislation;

- A repository of the voting patterns of MEPs with 'grades' for most of them, called "Political Memory" (negative grades being given to MEPs that voted against the amendment supported by La Quadrature, and positive grades to those that voted in favour);

---

[140] The Hadopi Law in France allows Internet Service Providers, when prompted, to cut off of Internet connections of repeat copyright offenders.

[141] This amendment was controversial as it was clearly aimed at prohibiting the Hadopi Law measures by making them illegal under EU law.

[142] See http://www.blackouteurope.eu/

[143] An avatar is a small image that is linked to your social media account (usually a picture of yourself or something you like, or a virtually created image of you).

[144] A wiki is collaborative website which can be directly edited by anyone with access to it. The most well-known wiki website is Wikipedia but anyone can easily create a wiki on the Internet.

- A directory with MEPs' contact details and example of phone call messages to use when contacting them[145], making it easy to mobilise their Followers to call when necessary (e.g. prior to a vote);

- A good working relationship with the mainstream press leading to numerous interviews, which were then posted on YouTube and Vimeo;

- A use of Twitter and similar tools to raise awareness and alert users to calls for action;

- A strong network of similar organisations across Europe allowing La Quadrature to (1) spread the word efficiently and (2) gain in terms of pan-European representativity; and,

- A physical presence in the corridors of the European Parliament.

The campaign led to an astonishing change of vote by several MEPs at the second reading vote on 6 May 2009, which in turn led to a third reading and a form of recognition of the existence of "net freedoms" under European law.

However, two mitigating factors must be highlighted regarding the result: (1) the timing of this debate played an important role because it happened only weeks away from the European elections, making MEPs more sensitive to 'word-on-the-street' pressure and (2) similar actions undertaken since then have led to MEPs complaining about being spammed by emails and calls. In short, the tactics that proved so successful then for La Quadrature are likely to be counter-productive when used in less urgent contexts.

**CAUTION
GOLDEN
RULES**

THE GOLDEN RULES TO A SUCCESSFUL ONLINE CAMPAIGN

Organising online campaigns should be done as a long-term project, conceived around four building blocks:

1. Engaging supporters, through a relevant and attractive use of the available online tools (short and visual often works best);
2. Building lists (whilst respecting privacy rules), so that every campaign widens the existing network;
3. Keeping the created community alive, through regular and preferably personal communications; and,
4. Evaluating outcomes on a regular basis: even the best ideas soundly realised could end up giving disappointing results, in which case it's not worth the effort.

---

[145] E.g. '(Hello my name is XY and I live in Z) I just sent you an email, have you read it? No? Let me tell you about it…'.

4.   Social Media to shape information

Journalists tend to rely increasingly on social media as an information source, as outlined by the study findings below. As a result, social media sources and comments are quoted more and more in mainstream news channels.

Social Media Importance

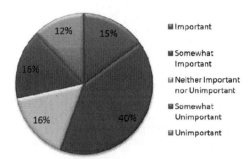

FIGURE 28-How important have social media become for reporting and producing the stories you write? – Source: GWU and Cision 2009 Social Media & Online Usage Study

In parallel, the European Parliament Digital Trends Study[146] by Fleishman Hillard released in May 2009 shows that 65 percent of MEPs visit Wikipedia-style information sources at least several times each week to understand legislative issues, while 36 percent visit blogs.

The combination of these trends means that influencing what appears on a Wikipedia page (either by creating Wikipedia pages on certain issues or editing existing pages to push one's vision forward) could become a major element in lobbying moving forward, as well as convincing influential bloggers to take a stance on a given policy issue.

---

[146] See http://www.epdigitaltrends.eu/

How frequently do you, or your staff on your behalf, use the following online tools/resources in your daily legislative work? (%)

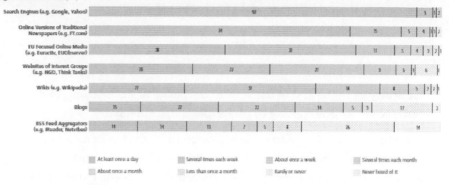

FIGURE 29- HOW ARE MEPS USING THE INTERNET TO UNDERSTAND LEGISLATIVE ISSUES –
SOURCE: FLEISHMAN HILLARD EP DIGITAL TRENDS 2009

I was unofficially told that even the European Commission is considering allocating some resources to "cleaning up" information on Wikipedia as they consider it in some cases to be biased or inaccurate, due to the ease with which anyone can edit a Wikipedia page. A battle of information (and disinformation) is therefore likely to increasingly take place on the Internet, as lobbyists, institutions and politicians try to influence the content available on sources such as Wikipedia.

OUTLOOK

This brings us to the end of our tour of the basics of EU lobbying, and the way in which social media is starting to play a role, albeit timidly.

But quite frankly, if lobbying is likely to keep the same basics moving forward, the impact of social media will evolve considerably over the next years, and has changed already quite substantially between the moment I started writing this book, and the moment I put the pen down (well, actually, the keyboard).

It is difficult to predict how the EU 2.0 landscape will evolve but online tools, regardless of what they are, are likely to continue taking a greater importance in the way the EU analyses dossiers, interacts with citizens (and lobbyists), and informs about what they do and think.

Mainstream politicians and lobbyists alike must accept the risks inherent to social media, as the benefits outweigh them by far, and use the available tools with common sense and a zest of paranoia.

This books sets out a certain number of Golden Rules and Tips but if there were only two things to remember they would be: whatever you do online or offline, stay true to yourself and make sure that you handle things ethically. This has a dual advantage: first, your sleep pattern can only be improved; secondly, it preserves your reputation as a lobbyist (or a politician, for that matter), which is after all your most valuable asset in Brussels (ranked just slightly higher than your intelligence).

To conclude: social media are likely to induce an evolution of lobbying and EU politics, not a revolution. Lobbying basics will remain the foundation that counts most: making use of them (and especially the 5Ps principle) will allow interest representatives to ensure they put all chances on their side when arguing a dossier before the EU institutions.

Lobbying is a valuable element in the decision-making process at EU level, when handled in a constructive and transparent manner, with the objective of bringing real-life and technical expertise to a debate too often handled from ivory towers.

PART 3:
ANNEXES

ANNEX 1 – THE BASICS OF THE EU: IMPACT OF THE LISBON TREATY

A. Before the Lisbon Treaty: The Three Pillars

The European Union

1st Pillar: the European Communities	2nd Pillar: Common Foreign and Security Policy	3rd Pillar: Cooperation in Justice and Home Affairs
• EC: - Customs Union and single market - Common Agricultural and Fisheries Policy - Competition law - Structural Policy - Trade Policy - EU citizenship - Education and culture -Trans-European networks - Consumer protection - Health - Research - Environment - Social Policy - Asylum Policy - External borders - Schengen Treaty -Immigration Policy Euratom & ECSC	• Foreign Policy: - Cooperation, common positions and measures - Human rights - Democracy - Aid to non-member countries Security Policy: - European Security and Defence Policy - EU battle groups - Peacekeeping and Disarmement	• Cooperation between judicial authorities in civil and criminal law - Police cooperation - Combating racism and xenophobia -Fighting the drugs and arms trades - Fighting organised crime - Criminal acts against children and trafficking in human beings - Fighting terrorism
Supranational Cooperation	Intergovernmental Cooperation	

THE TREATIES

FIGURE 30-THE 3 PILLARS PRIOR TO THE LISBON TREATY

The expression 'the Three pillars of the EU' was used prior to the entry into force of the Lisbon Treaty on 1 December 2009 to illustrate how the various forms of cooperation were built up within the EU, depending on which policy area and parts of the treaty provisions were involved.[147] They also reflected the fact that there were two separate entities, the European Community and the European Union, the latter having no legal character.

Each of the three pillars represented a different policy area, and were all held together by a common roof and common foundations.

The first pillar represented supranational cooperation, i.e. cooperation derived from the EC Treaty, which enabled the EU to issue legislation directly binding for EU Member States and citizens. In other terms, Member States had given up some of their sovereignty and EU institutions could act independently of the national governments.

Meanwhile, the second pillar represented foreign and security policy, while the third one covered intergovernmental cooperation relating to police and judicial cooperation in criminal matters.

The pillars' roof was made up by provisions common to the three policy areas, while the foundations were the provisions concerning treaty amendments, new member admission, and so on. With the entry into force of the Lisbon Treaty, however, the EU acquired a legal personality, and the distribution of competences ceased to fall under the "pillar structure".

Under the new Lisbon Treaty rules, the competences of the EU are classified as:

- Exclusive competences covering areas, in which the EU is solely competent to adopt Directives and conclude international agreements;
- Shared competences designating areas, which Member States cannot intervene in once the EU has already done so; and,
- Supported competences covering areas where the EU can intervene to support, coordinate or supplement Member States' actions.

---

[147] Old habits die hard: EU professionals and officials continue to refer to the pillars in many cases.

B. The Lisbon Treaty

1. Background

In 2001, a Declaration was issued after the Laeken Summit called for a Convention on the Future of Europe that would help simplify the EU Treaties and put forward the question of a possible EU Constitution.

This led to the signing of a Constitution in Rome in 2004, a document that never entered into force as it was rejected by the French and Dutch in referendums held in 2005.

After the failure of the proposed European Constitution, the Lisbon Treaty was officially signed by EU Heads of State and Government in Portugal on 13 December 2007, under German Council Presidency. The entry into force was delayed by a first rejection by the Irish in 2008, a "No" which was overturned in 2009 when a second referendum took place.

Constructed as a list of amendments of previous treaties, the first version of the Lisbon Treaty proved extremely difficult to read. A consolidated version is now available, revealing more clearly what major changes have been introduced at various levels.

2. Main Changes

Having been ratified by all 27 Member States, the Lisbon Treaty brought about the following main changes:

- The appointment of a permanent President of the European Council for a term of two and a half years, working in parallel with the six-month rotating EU Presidency by Member States. The Council President plays an interesting role as the 'agenda setter' of the European Councils, which bring together the Heads of State and Government.
- The creation of a High Representative for Foreign Affairs and Security Policy function, who is both a Vice-President of the Commission and the Chair of the External Affairs Council and merges the former functions of EU High Representative for Foreign Affairs and External Relations Commissioner.
- The attribution of a legal personality to the European Union, which allows it to formally sign Treaties, and the creation of a European diplomatic corps, the European External Action Service.

- A redistribution of voting weights of Member States within the Council.
- New powers for the European Commission and European Court of Justice, notably in the field of justice and home affairs.
- An extension of the co-decision procedure to 40 more legislative areas (including energy, intellectual property rights, fisheries, agriculture, and some aspects of justice and home affairs such as asylum, immigration, police cooperation and judicial cooperation in criminal matters), implying increased power for the European Parliament. This increase of power also applies to the Parliament's scrutiny over the Comitology procedure.
- An exit clause for Member States wishing to leave the European Union.
- More involvement by national parliaments with the ability for them to use an 'orange card' to jointly block a draft legislative act if they consider it to infringe the principle of subsidiarity.
- A mechanism allowing citizens to petition the Commission (the "European Citizen Initiative" or ECI).
- The entry of the Charter of Fundamental Rights into EU law (except for UK, Poland and the Czech Republic).
- Changes to the voting rules in Council, and more specifically the mechanism of Qualified Majority Voting (or QMV); and,
- Reduction of the number of Commissioners (from 27 to 15 by 2014 but with little clarity on how the transition is handled) and of MEPs (maximum of 750, with a minimum of 6 and a maximum of 96 per country, and an extra MEP squeezed in by Italy, hence the expression "750 plus one").

ANNEX 2 – UNDERSTANDING THE EP AGENDA

The EP agenda is an explosion of colours, each of which holds a specific meaning, both as regards the location and activities of MEPs, and the fact that a lobbyist badge grants you access or not (as lobbyists do not have access when MEPs are scheduled to attend plenary in Strasbourg) to the European Parliament buildings.

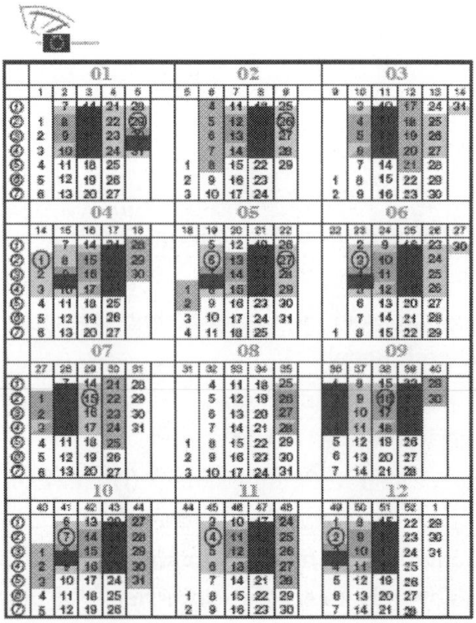

FIGURE 31-SCREENSHOT OF THE VERY COLOURFUL EP AGENDA

RED WEEKS = PLENARY SESSIONS

Usually in Strasbourg, except for the shorter sessions, which take place in Brussels.

These weeks run at the rhythm of the bell announcing at noon that MEPs need to vote.

MEPs vote on reports that have passed the Committee stage, adopt resolutions and put questions to the Commission and Council.

They have little time as their presence in plenary is often necessary (to vote) but occasionally use their free evenings to hit the town with the assistants. The EP building in Strasbourg is a secluded place and MEPs and assistants tend to be in the building most of the week, with assistants switching from hectic mode before the votes to relaxed mode once their MEP is in plenary.

BLUE WEEKS = POLITICAL GROUPS

These weeks usually take place just before plenary weeks, as they enable Political Groups to coordinate and formulate their positions for the assembly meeting with regards to agenda items. These meetings can take place in Brussels or elsewhere.

TURQUOISE/GREEN WEEKS = CONSTITUENCY

During these weeks, MEPs usually return to their constituency or are travelling.

These are usually good weeks to have a relaxed chat with assistants and political advisors, but don't even dream of finding an MEP (unless you try their constituency office).

PINK WEEKS = COMMITTEE

MEPs prepare the work voted on in plenary by 20 standing committees specialised in various areas. Committee weeks are usually very intense, seeing as many MEPs are members of more than one Committee. During Committee sessions, draft reports are voted on, updates on reports in progress are given, debates are held and own-initiative reports presented.

Annex 3 – Differences between the 3 Readings in Co-Decision

	FIRST READING	SECOND READING	THIRD READING / CONCILIATION
Timing	No time limits	Strict time limits of 3 to 4 months for EP and another max. 4 months for the Council	Max. 24 weeks (3 x 8 weeks), of which max. 8 weeks devoted to Conciliation as such
Who is responsible?	Committee responsible and Opinion-giving Committees	Only the Committee responsible	Primary responsibility lies with the Parliament Delegation to the Conciliation Committee
What is the basis of the Discussion?	Commission proposal	Common position	Council's Common Position and the EP's second reading amendments
Possibility to table amendments	Both at the Committee and the plenary stage (40 MEPs need to sign or Political Group)	Both at the Committee and the plenary stage (40 MEPs need to sign or Political Group)	No: approval or rejection of the joint text as a whole in a single vote
Admissibility criteria for amendments	Broad admissibility criteria for amendments	Strict admissibility criteria for amendments	No[148]
Required majority at plenary?	EP decides to either approve, reject or amend the Commission proposal by a *simple* majority (i.e. majority of MEPs voting)	EP approves the Common Position by a *simple* majority, but rejects or amends it by an *absolute* majority (i.e. majority of all MEPs)	EP approves or rejects the joint text by simple majority in a single vote

---

[148] This was established by the European Court of Justice (ECJ judgement of 10.1.2006 in the 'IATA' case), which ruled that Article 251 EC Treaty does not impose any restriction on the content of the measures chosen to help reach agreement on a joint text.

Annex 4 – EP Rules of procedures (RoP) on amendments

Generally speaking, the format of amendments depends on the nature of the text being amended (note the rules for tabling can change so it is always best to check regularly).

1. Amendments to legislative texts (in reports or opinions relating for example to a Directive) must always be to the original legislative text (and not, for example, to amendments tabled by the Rapporteur).

They are presented in the form of two columns. The relevant part of the text on which the Parliament is being consulted (i.e. usually the Commission proposal or the Common Position) appears in the left hand column. The proposed amendment to that text appears in the right-hand column. Any changes proposed in the amendment, compared with the original text, must be indicated in ***bold italics***.

- Additions are indicated in bold italics in text in the right-hand column.

- Deletions are indicated in bold italics in the legislative text on the left (and of course do not appear at all in the amendment on the right).

- If a whole section of the legislative text is to be removed, then it is shown (in bold italics) on the left and on the right the word **'(deleted)'** should appear in bold italics.

- If a new section is to be added, then nothing appears on the left and the proposed new text section appears (in bold italics) on the right

The illustration below shows how an amendment to a legislative text must look like for an MEP to table it.

EUROPEAN PARLIAMENT

2004   *2009*

Committee IMCO

12/03/2009   PE 421.119v02-00

AMENDMENTS [INSERT NUMBER]

Draft report   **(PE 421.119 v02-00)**
Rapporteur [Firstname Surname]
Title

Council common position for adopting a directive of the European Parliament and of the Council on amending Directive [Full name of text you are amending] (16497/1/2008 – C6-0068/2009 – 2007/0248(COD))

Amendment [LEAVE BLANK]
[Firstname Surname of MEP tabling amendment]

Council common position – **amending act**

Article 1 – point 21 bis (nouveau)
Directive 2002/22/CE
Article 32 bis (nouveau)
[LEAVE BLANK]
[LEAVE BLANK]

Text proposed	*Amendments by Parliament*
Insert text you intend to amend. Put in bold and italic elements changed by your amendment	**Insert your proposed version**. Put in bold and italic elements changed by your amendment

Or: en

Justification

Keep your justification short (max 500 characters)

2. In the case of **amendments to non-legislative texts** (e.g. an own-initiative report), the text that may be amended is the Rapporteur's motion for a resolution or the draftsman's draft opinion. Amendments are presented in a single column:

• Additions are indicated in bold italics;

- Deletions are indicated by the word **'*(deletion)*'** in bold italics;

- A completely new paragraph is to be marked **'*(new)*'** in bold italics; and,

- If a whole paragraph is deleted, this is to be marked, e.g.: 'Paragraph 6: *deleted*' in bold italics.

The illustration below shows how tabling amendments in this case is much simpler thanks to the single-column format (the heading would obviously be the same as previously, only the presentation of the amendment itself changing).

<u>Examples of amendments to NON-LEGISLATIVE texts</u>

Amendment by Karin Junker

Amendment 4
Citation 5b (new)

- *having regard to its resolution of 20 November 2002 on media concentration (P5_TA-PROV(2002)0554),*

Or. de

Amendment by Karin Junker

Amendment 5
Recital C

C. whereas the audiovisual sector is of fundamental importance for democracy, *diversity of opinion, pluralism and cultural diversity* and contributes to technological innovation, economic growth, the creation of jobs and the functioning of the single market,

Or. de

Annex 5 – EP Committee Voting List Example

The screenshot below shows what an EP Committee voting list looks like (see page 50 where we examine the role of EP Rapporteurs).

The abbreviations used in these voting lists are:

CA	Compromise amendment
CONS	Consolidated amendment
OA	Oral amendment
D	Deletion
SV	Split vote
pc	Corresponding part
W	Withdrawn
=	Identical amendments
(PR)	Draft recommendation

Subject of the amendment	Amendment number	Author	Rap-porteur Position	Voting indication	Re-marks	Result of vote
*Directive 20XX/XX/EC – [Name of Directive]*						
*Article 1* *[Heading of Article]*						
Article X – paragraph X *[subject in short]*	CA2	[name of MEP(s)]	+	**Put to vote** **Adoption CA2** ⇒ AM XXX falls. **Go to XX** Rejection CA1 ⇒ Go to XXX		+
	122	[name of MEP(s)]	–	Only put to vote if CA2 rejected		Falls
*Article 1* *[Heading of Article]*						
Article XX-XX	CA5 part 1	[name of MEP(s)]	+	**SV request by the [politi-cal party or MEP]** **Put CA 5 part 1 to vote** **Adoption CA5 part 1** ⇒ Except for AMs relating to recitals other than XX and XX referring to Art XX-XX and compatible with CA5, all other AMs to Art XX-XX, including AMs X, XX fall. **Go to CA5 part 2** **Rejection CA5 part 1** ⇒ CA5 part 2 falls. **Go to XX** *Part 1 consists of CA X except* *- Article XX, paragraph 1, point (b), 2nd indent*		+

Annex 6 – European Commission Amended Proposal Example

The screenshot below shows what a European Commission Amended Proposal looks like (see page 105 where we detail this step in the co-decision procedure).

Amended proposal for a

DIRECTIVE OF THE EUROPEAN PARLIAMENT AND OF THE COUNCIL

Amending Directive [Full name of Directive]

(Text with EEA relevance)

1.   **STAGE OF PROCEDURES**

The proposal – COM(20XX) XXX – 20XX/XXX (COD) – was adopted by the Commission on [date] and was sent to the European Parliament and to the Council on [date].

The European Economic and Social Committee adopted its opinion on the proposal from the Commission on [date].

The Committee of the Regions adopted its opinion on the Commission's proposal on [date].

The European Parliament adopted XXX amendments at first reading on [date].

2.   **OBJECTIVE OF THE PROPOSAL**

[+/- 15 lines]

3.   **OBJECTIVE OF THE AMENDED PROPOSAL**

The amended proposal adapts the original proposal on a number of points as suggested by the European Parliament.

4.   **OBSERVATIONS ON THE AMENDMENTS ADOPTED BY THE EUROPEAN PARLIAMENT**

4.1   **Amendments accepted by the Commission**

The Commission can accept amendments X, XX (except for 1ˢᵗ indent), XX (last paragraph), etc..

4.2   **Amendments accepted by the Commission in part or subject to rewording**

Amendments X, XX, etc.

–   Amendment X

The amendment clarifies XXXX The description needs, however, be revised in order to reflect the terms of Article XXX.

Recital 4 b (new)

[new text of amendment with additions underlined and deletions in strikethrough]

4.3.   **Amendments not accepted by the Commission**

Amendments X, XX (first paragraph), cannot be accepted by the Commission.

5.   **AMENDED PROPOSAL**

Having regard to Article 250(2) of the EC Treaty, the Commission amends its proposal as indicated above.

Annex 7 – Co-decision Third Reading Four-Column Document Example

The screenshot below shows what a four-column document used during the co-decision negotiations in third reading (conciliation) looks like (see page 115 where we detail conciliation).

If this view seems simple, it is because the columns are blank: imagine the same document filled with text, some of it in bold or in 'strikethrough' and parts of it highlighted in grey or yellow to attract the attention on the changes inserted.

In terms of the compromise proposal suggested by the Council rotating Presidency, the usual recommendations are:

- Keep common position;
- CA (for compromise amendment) n°XX is acceptable for this paragraph;
- AM (for amendment) XX is acceptable; or,
- An alternative amendment trying to reconcile the different positions.

[name of] DIRECTIVE			
	COUNCIL COMMON POSITION [Date of CP]	**EUROPEAN PARLIAMENT'S** Recommendation voted [date] or proposed at trialog [date] (before tabling office verification)	**COMPROMISE PROPOSAL** in relation to EP voted text
1.1. *RECITALS*			
			Typical types of recommendations: • Keep common position. • CA (for compromise amendment) n°XX is acceptable for this paragraph. • AM (for amendment) XX is acceptable • An alternative amendment trying to reconcile the different positions
Article 1			
Article 2 *Definitions*			
ANNEX I			

Annex 8 – Short Social Media Glossary

Aggregator: A Web application or programme that retrieves news (syndication) feeds from other sources and combines them (by topic, preference, randomly, etc) potentially sorting them by date, title, author or topic.

Akismet Comment spam filter popular with Wordpress blogs.

Astroturfing A fake grassroots push to generate buzz or interest in a product, service, or idea.

Avatar A graphical image or likeness that replaces a photo of the author of the content on a blog.

Badge A (usually square) image displayed on a blog, which signifies the blogger's participation in an event, contest, or social movement

Blog (short for *"Web log"*) A website where individual(s) provide entries of any type of content from videos and podcasts to traditional text and photos in order to inform or create discussions. The entries are presented in reverse chronological order.

Blogosphere Collective term encompassing all blogs and their interconnections, the idea being that blogs exist together as a connected community.

Blog Post/Entry Content published on a blog. Entries may include pictures or embedded videos and links URLs for online sources used.

Blogroll A list of blogs (including the link to them) that appears on a blog site, typically as a recommendation by the blogger of the other blogs he is most influenced by.

Bounce Rate (1) The percentage visitors who only visit the home page of a website and then leave immediately.

(2) The percentage of emails which never reach their intended recipient (usually due to the fact the email address is no longer valid).

Brand Reach Number of individuals exposed to a brand or product in a given period.

Categories	Pre-specified keywords for organising content; form part of a taxonomy.
Champions	Group of enthusiasts who post messages, reply to other bloggers and provide information in order to get the online community moving and conversations started.
Comments	Replies or opinions in reference to blog entries, debates or hot topics; usually left on blog posts.
Crowd-sourcing	Refers to organisations harnessing the skills and enthusiasm of Internet users not part of the organisation who are prepared to volunteer their time contributing content and solving problems.
Dashboard	The administration area on your blog software which allows you to post, check traffic, upload files, manage comments, etc.
Delicious	Property of Yahoo!, this social bookmarking site allows users to quickly store, organise (by tags) and share favourite web pages. You can also subscribe to RSS feeds of other users and share a page specifically with another user.
Digg	Digg is a place for people to discover, share and recommend content from anywhere on the web.
"Do-good" networks	Online communities aimed at making the world a better place.
Flickr	The largest photography social networking site on in the Internet. Flickr has more than three billion photographs online, with three million to five million new photographs added daily. Vancouver-based Ludicorp started the service in 2004, and Yahoo! acquired it in 2005.
Folksonomy (*also known as social or collaborative tagging, social classification, social indexing*)	The practice and method of collaboratively creating and managing tags to annotate and categorize content. Folksonomy describes the bottom-up classification systems that emerge from social tagging.

Geo-Marketing	Using geographical intelligence in marketing from sales to distribution.
Google Alerts	Service offered by search engine company Google which notifies its users by email or as a feed about the latest web and news pages of their choice.
Hashtags	A community-driven convention for adding additional context and meta data to your tweets. They are created simply by prefixing a word with a hash symbol: #hashtag.
Information Cloud	"People in the machine nurture the cloud." Is a quote by Dion Hinchcliffe, one of the so-called gurus of web 2.0. Refers to the accumulation of information in the network and the fact that every person blogging, tweeting or collaborating via social networks feeds into the information cloud on the Internet.
Information Overload	Information overload refers to an excess amount of information being provided, making processing and absorbing tasks very difficult for the individual.
Instant Messaging	Any system that allows instantaneous person-to-person conversations over a network, and has its root in 1960s early Unix chat systems.
IRL	In real life; that is, face to face as opposed to via a computer network.
Life-streaming	The practice of collecting an online user's disjointed online presence in one central location rather than spread across the web on Flickr, YouTube, Facebook and Twitter. There are third-party services that aggregate the content from your various social websites and display such content in chronological order. (FriendFeed, Tumblr.com and Sweetcron).
LinkedIn	One of the first business-oriented social networking companies, founded in 2002 and currently supporting more than 70 million registered users across 150 industries.
Maven	A trusted expert in a particular field, who seeks to pass knowledge on to others. 'Maven' is a Yiddish term and

means 'one who accumulates knowledge'.

Message Boards / Forums	An online discussion site: people who want to discuss particular issues or need support post threads (a message) on the forum or message board to gain more information or start a conversation.
Meta Tags	Text inserted into the code of a web page which includes keywords for search engine optimisation and handicapped persons.
Metcalfe's Law	The value of a network is proportional to the number of connected users.
Micro-blogging	A form of blogging where the entries/posts are limited to a certain amount of characters or words, i.e. Twitter.
Micro-philanthropy	Donating in small amounts (€1, €2, €5, €10).
Multimedia	Media and content in different forms such as videos, pictures, etc. Examples include YouTube and Flickr.
New Media	New media is a term meant to encompass the emergence of digital, computerised, or networked information and communication technologies in the later part of the 20th century.
News Feed	A document containing both information about the provider of the feed and a collection of entries, each of which provides publishing information about a given blog or similar article, including summary and categorisation information.
Online Identity Management	Also known as online image management or online personal branding, this is a set of methods for generating a distinguished Web presence of a person on the Internet. That presence could be reflected in any kind of content that refers to the person, including news, participation in blogs and forums, personal web site, social media presence, pictures, video, etc.
Online Reputation Management	Consistent research and analysis of one's personal or professional, business or industry reputation as represented by the content across all types of online

(ORM)	media. It is also sometimes referred to as Online Reputation Monitoring, maintaining the same acronym. The objective of online identity management is to maximise the appearances of positive online references about a specific person, targeting not only to users that actively search for that person on any Search Engine, but also to those that eventually can reach a person's reference while browsing the web, and to solve online reputation problems.
OpenID	An open standard protocol for performing authentication on an OpenID participant by referencing a corresponding authentication provider. Because it is an open standard, OpenID is being rapidly adopted across the Web as a means to create a 'single sign-on', reducing the number of user names and passwords a person needs to remember and thereby making signing in easier and quicker.
Opinion Leaders	Change agents and opinion leaders often play major roles in spurring the adoption of innovations, although factors inherent to the innovations also play a role.
Participation Culture	When people use social media to share and collaborate. It may encourage openness and transparency. However, the tools themselves do not create a participatory culture.
Personal Cloud	Accumulation of data and Web services you wish to use, with information that is important to you. May include your calendar, email, Facebook Account, Images, Flickr, Gmail, News Feeds, Twitter Feeds, Blogroll, etc...
Podcast	A specialised form of blog post that points to a streaming media file instead of a Web page. Podcasts (audio files) take their name from the Apple iPod. Vidcasts or Vlogs are the video equivalent of podcasts.
Reach	The degree to which any member of a network is able to reach other members of the network.

Reputation Management	Focuses on managing brand, product, or personal perceptions through an active, near real-time programme of conscious engagement in social media outlets.
RSS *(stands for Really Simple Syndication)*	One of the earliest syndication feed formats. A syndication feed for a Web or blogging site contains recent changes (new articles, revisions to existing articles, additional media and so forth) that is read by a syndication client.
RSS Readers	RSS readers aggregate all of your social networking messages, as well as news and blog posts into one place in real time.
SEO *(stands for Search-Engine Optimisation)*	The process of configuring Web content in order to gain the highest potential rankings for a given search engine. While early SEO systems involved simple keyword matches, SEO has evolved considerably, to the level of (1) performing semantic searches on content, (2) optimising the specific layout of a page to make its terms more indexable, and (3) using complex mathematical algorithms to better match anticipated search engine behaviours.
Sidebar	A column (or multiple columns) along either or both sides of a blog site's main content area. The sidebar often includes contact information about the author, a blog mission statement, as well as categories, links to archives, honour badges (e.g. Best Blog in 2010) and other widgets the author includes on the site.
Social Bookmarking	A method for people to search, organise, store and share items (i.e. blog posts, online articles, pictures, etc.) by using the item's URL.
Social Interaction Overload	Too much social interaction.
Social Media Optimisation (SMO)	Set of methods for generating publicity through social media, online communities and community websites. Methods of SMO include adding RSS feeds, social news

buttons, blogging, and incorporating third-party community functionalities like images and videos.

Social Networking   The process of creating relationships between a user and other people based upon some formal social graph. Social networks can be thought of as communities linked through interests or commonality and which use the Internet to connect network members. Typically contains points of presence (avatars), blogs, Web forums and micro-formats.

Social Web   Describes how people socialise or interact with each other throughout the World Wide Web, usually brought together through a variety of shared interests.

Social Capital: A sociology concept also used in business, economics, organisational behaviour, political science, public health and natural resources management. Refers to connections within and between social networks, as well as connections among individuals.

Small   World Phenomenon   The small world experiment comprised several experiments conducted by Stanley Milgram examining the average path length for social networks of people in the United States. The research was groundbreaking in that it suggested that human society is a small world type network characterised by short path lengths. The experiments are often associated with the phrase "six degrees of separation", although Milgram did not use this term himself.

Tagging   The process of adding categorical information (usually one word or simple two-word phrases) which identifies some aspect of a Web resource. For instance, a picture of a European Commissioner may include tags for "EU," "Brussels," "Commissioner," "European Commission" and so forth.

Trackback   Some blogs provide a facility for other bloggers to leave an automated calling card, instead of commenting. Blogger A may write on blog A about an item on blogger B's site, and through the trackback facility leave a link on B's site back to A. The collection of

	comments and trackbacks on a site facilitates conversations.
Troll	Someone who becomes obsessed and deeply offended by everything you write on your blog and who goes onto other sites to badmouth you and put a link up to your blog. This can actually be helpful to you in the long run in terms of inbound links. Usually, they are quite annoying however.
Tweet-Up *(also called "Twunch" if at lunch time)*	Organised Twitter face-to-face meet-up at a local restaurant, club or elsewhere.
Twitter	A microblogging platform created by Obvious in 2005, where users send short (under 140 characters) messages–called tweets–to subscribers of a given person's Twitter feed.
User Generated Content (UGC)	User-generated content, also known as consumer-generated media (CGM) or user-created content (UCC), refers to various kinds of media content, publicly available, that are produced by end-users.
Web 2.0	Second generation of Web development and design that facilitates communication, secure information sharing, interoperability, and collaboration on the World Wide Web. Web 2.0 concepts have led to the development and evolution of web-based communities, hosted services, and applications; such as social-networking sites, video-sharing sites, wikis, blogs, and folksonomies.
Webinar	An online seminar.
Widgets	Stand-alone applications you can embed in other applications, like a website or a desktop, or view on its own on a PDA or smart phone. These may help you to do things like subscribe to a feed, do a specialist search, or even make a donation.
Wiki	Webpage(s) used to collect content about a topic. Anyone with access can edit, modify or delete the information.

REFERENCES

Benedetto, Giacomo (2005). 'Rapporteurs as legislative entrepreneurs: the dynamics of the codecision procedure in Europe's parliament' in: *Journal of European Public Policy*, Vol. 12 (1): pp. 67-88.

Beyers, Jan (2004): 'Voice and Access. Political practices of European interest associations' in: *European Union Politics*, Vol. 5(2): pp. 211-240.

Binderkrantz, Anne (2003). 'Strategies of Influence: How Interest Organizations React to Changes in Parliamentary Influence and Activity' in: *Scandinavian Political Studies*, Vol. 26 (4): pp. 287-306.

Bouwen, Pieter (2002). *Comparative Study of Business Lobbying in the European Parliament, the European Commission and the Council of Ministers*. Max Planck Institute for the Study of Societies Discussion Paper 02/7. Köln.

Bouwen, Pieter (2003): 'A Theoretical and Empirical Study of Corporate Lobbying in the European Parliament' in: *European Integration online Papers*, Vol. 7(11). See http://eiop.or.at/eiop/texte/2003-011a.htm

Bowler, Shaun and Farrell, David M. (1995). 'The Organizing of the European Parliament: Committees, Specialization and Co-Ordination' in: *British Journal of Political Science*, Vol. 25 (2): pp. 219-243.

Burns, Charlotte (2004). 'Codecision and the European Commission: a study of declining influence?' in: *Journal of European Public Policy*, Vol. 11(1): pp. 1-18.

Burson-Marsteller (2009). *A guide to Effective Lobbying in Europe*. See http://www.burson-marsteller.eu/newsletter/effective_lobbying/2009/index.html

Carney, Eliza Newlin (2009). 'All a-Twitter' in: *National Journal*, 3/21/09, pp. 52-53.

Coen, David (2007). 'Empirical and theoretical studies in EU lobbying' in: *Journal of European Public Policy*, Vol. 14(3): pp. 333-345.

Corbett, Richard; Jacobs, Francis and Shackleton, Michael (2005). *The European Parliament*. Sixth Edition. London.

Coultrap, John (1999). 'From Parliamentarism to Pluralism: Models of Democracy and the European Union's 'Democratic Deficit'' in: *Journal of Theoretical Politics*, Vol. 11(1): 107-135.

Delany, Colin (2008). *Online Politics 101*. Version 1.5/June 2008. See http://www.epolitics.com

Delany, Colin (2009). *Learning from Obama: Lessons for Online Communicators in 2009 and Beyond*. See http://www.epolitics.com

Denzin, Norman K. and Lincoln, Yvonna S. (1998). *Strategies of Qualitative Enquiry*. Thousand Oaks et al.

Donnelly, Brendan (2007). The European Union after the European Reform Treaty.   See http://www.federalunion.org.uk/news/2007/070909reformtreaty.shtml

Eising, Rainer (2007). 'The access of business interests to EU institutions: towards elite pluralism?' in: *Journal of European Public Policy*, Vol. 14(3): pp. 384-403.

European Commission (2009). *Your Guide to the Lisbon Treaty*. Brussels.

European Parliament (2007). *Conciliation and Codecision, a Guide to how the Parliament co-legislates*. Brussels.

Farrell, Henry and Héritier, Adrienne (2004). *Inter-organizational Negotiation and Intraorganizational Power in Shared Decision-Making. Early agreements of Ministers*. Vienna.

Fink-Hafner, Danica and Krasovec, Alenka (2005). 'Is Consultation Everything? The Influence of Interest Groups on Parliamentary Working Bodies in Slovenia' in: *Czech Sociological Review*, Vol. 41 (3): pp. 401-421.

Fleishman Hillard (2009). *European Parliament Digital Trends*. See: http://www.epdigitaltrends.eu/

Follesdal, Andreas (2005). 'Towards a stable finalité with federal features? The balancing acts of the Constitutional Treaty for Europe' in: *Journal of European Public Policy*, Vol. 12 (3): pp. 572-589.

Fondation Robert Schuman (2007). *The Lisbon Treaty – 10 easy-to-read fact sheets*.

Garman, Julie and Hilditch, Louise (1998). 'Behind the scenes: an examination of the importance of the informal processes at work in conciliation' in: *Journal of European Public Policy*, Vol. 5 (2): pp. 271-284.

Geiger, Andreas (2006). *EU Lobbying Handbook. A guide to modern participation in Brussels*. Berlin.

Godin, Seth. *Brainwashed: seven ways to reinvent yourself*. In: Change This No 66.01.

Grayling (2009). *Your Business Guide to the Treaty of Lisbon: What Changes? What is the impact on business and lobbying?*. Brussels.

Greenwood, Justin (2007). *Interest Representation in the European Union*. New York.

Hagemann, Sara (2009). 'Strength in numbers? An evaluation of the 2004-209 European Parliament', in: *EPC Issue Paper No.58*.

Harris, Tom (2010). *Top Ten Tips for political bloggers*. See: http://www.tomharris.org.uk/2010/02/10/top-ten-tips-for-political-bloggers/

Héritier, Adrienne (2003). 'Composite democracy in Europe: the role of transparency and access to information' in: *Journal of European Public Policy*, Vol. 10 (5): pp. 814-833.

Héritier, Adrienne (2007). *Explaining Institutional Change in Europe*. New York.

Hilson, Chris (2002): 'New social movements: the role of legal opportunity' in: *Journal of European Public Policy*, Vol. 9(2): pp. 238-255.

Hix, Simon; Raunio, Tapio and Scully, Roger (1999). 'An Institutional Theory of Behaviour in the European Parliament'. EPRG Working Paper, No. 1. Presented at the Joint Sessions of the European Consortium for Political Research, 26-31 March 1999, Mannheim: See http://www.lse.ac.uk/collections/EPRG/pdf/Working%20Paper%201.pdf

Hix, Simon (2005). *The Political System of the European Union*. Second Edition. London, New York.

Hix, Simon (2009). 'What to expect in the 2009-2014 European Parliament: Return of the grand Coalition' in: *European Policy Analysis*, issue 8-2009, pp. 1-12.

Hix, Simon and Benedetto, Giacomo (2007). 'Explaining the European Parliament's gains in the EU Constitution' in: *Review of International Organization*, Vol. 2(2): pp. 115-129.

Hojnacki, Marie and Kimball, David C. (1998). 'Organized Interests and the Decision of Whom to Lobby in Congress' in: *The American Political Science Review*, Vol. 92(4): pp. 775- 790.

Ireland, Emilienne and Tajitsu Nash, Phil (2001). *Winning Campaigns Online*. Science Writers Press. Bethesda.

Judge, David and David Earnshaw (2003). *The European Parliament*. Ebbw Vale, New York.

Kohler-Koch, Beate (1997). 'Organized Interests in the EC and the European Parliament' in: *European Integration online Papers (EIoP)*, Vol. 1(9). See http://eiop.or.at/eiop/texte/1997-009a.htm

Kreppel, Amie (2003). 'Necessary but not sufficient: understanding the impact of treaty reform on the internal development of the European Parliament' in: *Journal of European Public Policy*, Vol. 10(6): pp. 884-911.

Lahusen, Christian (2002). 'Commercial consultancies in the European Union: the shape and structure of professional interest intermediation' in: *Journal of European Public Policy*, Vol. 9(5): pp. 695-714.

Leary, Brent and Bullock, David (2008). *Barack Obama's Social Media Lessons for Business with Interactive Online Companion*. Lulu.com.

Linkfluence (2009). 'European political web: a study of EU politics on the social web', Oct-Nov 2009. See: http://us.linkfluence.net/2009/11/20/first-map-of-the-eurosphere/

Mahoney, Christine (2004). 'The Power of Institutions. State and Interest Group Activity in the European Union' in: *European Union Politics*. Vol. 5(4): pp. 441-466.

Mahoney, Christine (2007). 'Networking vs. allying: the decision of interest groups to join coalitions in the US and the EU' in: *Journal of European Public Policy*, Vol. 14(3): pp. 366- 383.

Marziali, Valeria (2006). *Lobbying in Brussels. Interest Representation and Need for Information*. Discussion Paper. Bonn.

Mazey, Sonia and Richardson, Jeremy (1996). 'The logic of organisation: Interest groups' in: Richardson, Jeremy (eds.). European Union. Power and Policy-Making. London and New York: pp. 200-216.

Michalowitz, Irina (2005). 'Assessing Conditions for Influence of Interest Groups in the EU' in: *Political Science Series*, Vol.106. Vienna.

Nielsen (2009). *Global Faces and Networked Places – A Nielsen Report on Social Networking's New Global Footprint*.

Panagopoulos, Costas (2009). *Politicking Online*. Rutgers University Press. London.

Pollack, Mark A. (1997). 'Representing diffuse interests in EC policy-making' in: *Journal of European Public Policy*, Vol. 4(4): pp. 572-590.

PSB (2009), *EU lobbying: summary of results*. See: http://www.burson-marsteller.de/images/upload/eulobbyingresults_040909.pdf

Safko, Lon and Brake, David K. (2009), *The Social Media Bible*. John Wiley. Hoboken.

Schendelen, Rinus van (2005). *Machiavelli in Brussels. The Art of Lobbying in the EU*. Amsterdam.

Scott, David (2007). *The New Rules of Marketing & PR*. John Wiley. Hoboken.

Shackleton, Michael and Raunio, Tapio (2003). 'Codecision since Amsterdam: a laboratory for institutional innovation and change' in: *Journal of European Public Policy*, Vol. 10 (2): pp. 171-188.

Solis, Brian. *The Future of Communications – A Manifesto for Integrating Social Media into Marketing*.

Spencer, Tom (2004). 'Of Change, Training and Public Affairs in Europe' in: *Journal of Public Affairs*.

Stacey, Jeffrey (2003). 'Displacement of the Council via informal dynamics? Comparing the Commission and Parliament' in: *Journal of European Public Policy*, Vol. 10(6): pp. 936-955.

Taylor, Simon (2007). 'The place to be?' in: *European Voice*, Vol.13 (41). See http://www.europeanvoice.com/archive/article.asp?id=29241

Woll, Cornelia (2006). 'Lobbying in the European Union: From sui generis to a comparative perspective' in: *Journal of European Public Policy*, Vol. 13(3): pp. 456-469.

Zetter, Lionel (2008). *Lobbying – The Art of Political Persuasion*. Hampshire.